炭火焼き

lonely planet

BEST IN TRAVEL 2027

THE 50 BEST DESTINATIONS AND EXPERIENCES FOR THE YEAR AHEAD

CONTENTS

Destinations

Experiences

Introduction

Left: Threading from the Côte d'Azur and Provence to Grenoble in the French Alps, the Route Napoleon offers tempting side trips like Gorges du Verdon, home to burgeoning birdlife, eagles'-nest ancient chapels and fascinating prehistory.

The best trips always end with a great story.

The detour taken on instinct. The life-changing meal. The change in plans because of a recommendation from someone you met that was too good to miss. These are the moments that stay with us – not because they were perfect, but because they were unexpected. At Lonely Planet we've always believed that great travel requires space for serendipity.

Best in Travel 2027 is about finding your own story.

We love giving you the confidence to explore, wander and say 'yes' to the unexpected. You'll see that we love the world's most iconic places just as much as we believe in the excitement of finding unique experiences. The two aren't opposites – in fact, the most memorable journeys often happen when the familiar and the unanticipated meet.

Some of the highlights of this book are instantly recognizable: a polar plunge in Antarctica or an enchanted hike among California's coastal redwoods. Others – like a slow summer on the Swedish Riviera or the shimmering glass-and-gold skyline of Kazakhstan's capital – might (we hope) feel like surprising picks. All of them reward curiosity. They're places where arriving with an open mind makes all the difference. There are cities like Chengdu in China that reveal themselves, neighborhood by neighborhood. Landscapes like Tanzania's Gombe National Park that invite you to slow down and take notice. Local experiences like those in Šibenik, Croatia, where the richest immersion often comes from following local rhythms rather than rigid itineraries.

The experiences we've chosen work the same way. They aren't about chasing extremes or collecting bragging rights – they're about immersion and allowing for chance encounters and unplanned moments to shape your journey. These are experiences that don't rush you through; they invite you in.

Every recommendation in *Best in Travel 2027* is rooted in lived experience, told by someone who either traveled there or lives there. We hope they will make you feel confident enough to look around, ask questions and embrace the moment you're in as deeply as you can.

Travel in 2027 isn't about doing more, it's about being present in a world that's always on. It's about standing still to disconnect and take it all in when a million things are competing for your attention. It's about choosing places and experiences that give you the freedom to explore on your own terms, while still feeling supported by trusted experts. That balance – between guidance and openness – is where serendipity thrives.

Best in Travel 2027 is both a guide and an invitation. A guide shaped by decades of knowledge and lived experiences, and an invitation to travel with curiosity, humility and trust. A way to explore the world, connect with the people you meet and experience in full the unexpected stories waiting to unfold.

—NITYA CHAMBERS, EXECUTIVE EDITOR

DESTINATIONS

BEACHES AND RYŪKYŪAN CULTURE IN SOUTHERNMOST JAPAN

Okinawa, Japan

SELENA TAKIGAWA HOY If you haven't been to Okinawa, it's understandable; Japan's southernmost prefecture is a three-hour flight from Tokyo and off the easy shinkansen (bullet train) circuit. But reconsider and you'll discover what most Japanese people already know: that this chain of islands is a subtropical paradise with a distinct culture, resplendent nature and a laid-back atmosphere that relieves the stress of high-strung mainlanders.

The 160 islands of Okinawa Prefecture stretch like beads on a necklace from Kyūshū towards Taiwan, glinting like emeralds on cerulean silk. Just 49 of these are inhabited, starting with Okinawa Island – seat of the capital Naha. The majority of the prefecture's 1.4 million residents live on this island, which unrolls from the densely populated south to the wild, UNESCO World Heritage Site of Yambaru National Park in the north, thickly forested and sparsely populated – by humans at least.

I spent an evening in Yambaru kayaking through the park's mangroves under dark skies, led by a naturalist guide who explained the ecological importance of these entwined networks of hardy coastal trees, which cleanse the water and shore up the land. He pointed out crabs and mudskippers that skimmed the surface as fireflies winked to life, mirroring the starry sky above.

Nature is special across the archipelago: the endangered Iriomote cat stalks the forests of the Iriomote-Ishigaki National Park in the Yaeyama Islands; pineapple and papaya grow here to sweeten local meals; manta rays and sea turtles swim amongst vibrant coral colonies just offshore. I first learned to snorkel at Blue Cave on Okinawa Island's Cape Maeda, tentatively paddling through the protected pools as the undersea life revealed itself fish by fish. As I entered the limestone cavern of Blue Cave itself, the light changed, abruptly transforming a bright summer morning to an otherworldly outing as parrotfish, morays and titan triggerfish glimmered under the sapphire surface.

In the winter, humpback whales mate and raise their young among the Kerama Islands, breaching and splashing in playful pods. If you're lucky, you might spot the flightless Okinawa rail or the serene manatee-like dugong – both endangered species that call this island chain home.

Previous pages: Indigenous Ryūkyū dancers, resplendent in colorful kimonos. *Left:* Tropical perfection awaits at the Yaeyama Islands' Iriomote-Ishigaki National Park. *Above:* Okinawa's lilting *min'yō* (folk music) is accompanied by the three-stringed *sanshin* (lute).

DON'T LEAVE WITHOUT ...

1. Snorkeling turquoise-blue seas to marvel at coral reefs and, perhaps, to spot manta rays and sea turtles.

2. Sampling local delicacies like citrusy *shikuwasa* juice; purple *beni imo* (sweet potatoes); *gōya champuru*, a stir-fried dish with bitter melon, tofu and Spam; and *umi budo* (sea grapes; a kind of seaweed) that burst like caviar on the tongue.

3. Visiting some of the relics of the Ryūkyū Kingdom, like the 14th-century stronghold of Shuri-jō or ruined Nakagusuku-jō.

Right: The seaside Shintō shrine of Naminoue-gū in Naha, capital of Okinawa Prefecture. *Above left:* SUPs offer a gentle way to explore the limpid waters off Okinawa Island. *Above right:* Quiet streets in tiny Taketomi Island, part of the remote Yaeyama group

History buffs will find much to see too, like the castles and ruins of the Ryūkyū Kingdom, which ruled these islands for over 400 years from 1429 to 1872, before the Empire of Japan conquered the state and brought it under Japanese rule. On one visit, I joined a yoga class at Nakagusuku-jō, stretching out alongside waving grasses next to the graceful stone walls that are all that remain of this ancient fortress. The castle park is perched on a hill, offering regal views overlooking the surrounding town and out to the sea. More recently, Okinawa was the site of a number of the most grueling battles of the Pacific War during WWII; monuments and remnants of fighting and resistance are still scattered across the prefecture.

For a glimpse of Indigenous Ryūkyū culture, don't miss the folk art. You'll spot *shīsā* (ceramic guardian lion-dogs) perched on most roofs or at the entrances to homes and businesses. There's also *bingata*, the colorful resist-dyed fabrics with motifs of nature and the sea; they're seen on kimonos, especially during festival season. And my favorite of all is *min'yō* (folk music), lilting and plaintive and accompanied by the three-stringed *sanshin* (lute). To hear it is to be transported to a seaside village – you may not want to leave.

CURIOUS ADVENTURES

AROUND EVERY TURN

New Mexico, USA

JOEL BALSAM Touch down in New Mexico (spaceship optional) and gear up for a Southwestern road trip that feels like time travel and cosmic adventure rolled into one – from thriving Native American cultures and echoes of Wild West shoot-outs to explosively flavorsome cuisine and Martian-worthy landscapes, above and below ground. The only thing New Mexico's missing? Crowds.

New Mexico has always had a mysterious gravitational pull for the curious wanderer. Dinosaurs trudged through here 100 million years ago, and you can still trace their steps at Clayton Lake State Park. Some of the earliest humans in North America also roamed this land – 23,000-year-old fossilized footprints were uncovered at White Sands National Park, a bizarre desert-like place with towering 60ft-high (18m) dunes of white gypsum crystals. New Mexico has drawn artists like Georgia O'Keeffe and DH Lawrence, as well as Wild West antihero Billy the Kid, ski bums, Robert Oppenheimer and his team of wartime nuclear researchers and – yes – tiny green Martians if you buy into the Roswell lore.

What is it about this quiet Southwestern state that's so magnetic? Is it the pink sunsets and endless sky? Maybe it's the mix of Indigenous, Latino and Anglo-American cultures that blend together like the intricate geometric patterns of a Southwestern fleece?

New Mexico first pulled me in while driving across the United States in a 1987 Chevy RV. I didn't know what to expect. What I encountered was a place rich in experiences – yet with few other visitors. Was this one of the country's most incredible, underappreciated states, or was I drinking too many prickly-pear margaritas? Find out for yourself in 2027.

Hop in your flying saucer – a regular car will do – and set off on a road trip through enchanted landscapes. Get your kicks on a chunk of Route 66, the US's most iconic

Previous pages: Otherworldly hoodoos in the Bisti/De-Na-Zin Wilderness Area, New Mexico. *Left:* Albuquerque's burbs, overlooked by the Sandia Mountains. *Above: Blue Coyote* by Don Kennell (Lead Artist) and Dylan Kendall (Artist) announces Meow Wolf Santa Fe's House of Eternal Return, where interactive art meets amateur sleuthing.

highway, fresh off its 100th anniversary and spruced up with restored neon signs, new murals and updated visitor amenities across the eight states it swings through. Or travel the Turquoise Trail between Albuquerque and Santa Fe to see ghost towns Madrid and Los Cerrillos, plus the quirky Tinkertown Museum – home to thousands of folk-art miniatures created over four decades by the late Ross Ward 'while you were watching TV.'

Santa Fe can claim to be New Mexico's prettiest city – and maybe the country's. Wandering among its enchanting Pueblo Revival adobe-style houses feels like visiting a giant live-in gallery. Don't miss the Georgia O'Keeffe Museum and Meow Wolf – part gallery, part mystery, part psychedelic odyssey. Getting to the state capital will be easier in 2027, with new or expanded routes from Los Angeles, Chicago and Las Vegas, along with additions to the Santa Fe Regional Airport.

Albuquerque – New Mexico's biggest city and home to its best-connected airport (Albuquerque Sunport). Catch a show at the historic KiMo Theatre – turning 100 in 2027. Or float above the Sandia Mountains at the 55th Balloon Fiesta, the world's largest hot-air balloon festival, in October.

Wherever you go, leave some time for spontaneous side quests – you never know where New Mexico's next enticing curiosity might steer you.

Left: Explore an otherworldly Sahara in the US Southwest at the glistening gypsum-crystal dunes of White Sands National Park. *Above:* New Mexico's marvelous red chiles strung out to dry in Albuquerque

DON'T LEAVE WITHOUT ...

1. Meeting members of New Mexico's many Indigenous communities – from a clifftop mesa in Acoma and the just-as-ancient Taos Pueblo to Albuquerque's Indian Pueblo Cultural Center.

2. Tasting Frito pie, burritos smothered in New Mexico's proud green- or red-chile sauce, and prickly-pear margaritas (but take it easy, unlike this writer).

3. Exploring the state's natural wonders, from Carlsbad Caverns National Park to humongous hoodoos at Bisti/De-Na-Zin Wilderness Area.

THE UNSUNG HERO OF DALMATIA

Šibenik, Croatia

LUCIE GRACE The ornate yet quaint cobblestone alleys of Šibenik's Old Town ooze with both Adriatic elegance and local Croatian charm. Architectural marvels, gastronomic delights and cultural tradition are the MO, but it's not all antiquated vibes here – this pint-sized city is hip and lively, with festivals punctuating the year.

When people ask me where to go in Croatia, I recommend Šibenik without fail. This perennially popular country certainly has more celebrated destinations along its 1104-mile-long (1777km) stretch of coastline, but there's something special about Šibenik. Perhaps above all else, it's that this place feels like a local secret – it's still relatively off the tourist trail, tucked between Split and Zadar in a fortified alcove on the Dalmatian stretch of the Adriatic Sea.

For me, nothing beats a sunset stroll along Šibenik's seaside Riva promenade, passing seafood restaurants and cocktail bars before taking the sweeping stairs up to the majestic, UNESCO-listed St James Cathedral; its striking white marble, mined from nearby island Brač, dazzles whether floodlit by night or in the daytime sunlight. The cathedral is layered with architectural styles from its Gothic- and Renaissance-era heydays, emblematic of the city's rich history: Šibenik was a powerful medieval maritime trading hub, later conquered by the Venetian Republic.

But it's the 42,000 locals that set the city apart from neighboring destinations – the Old Town is very lived-in and lacks hectic tourist crowds, so while being uncommonly pretty, there's also the normalcy of everyday life here. But don't mistake Šibenik for a sleepy old burg; there's a lot going on for visitors too.

If you come in June you may well stumble across some puppetry, theater or arts on the streets as the heartwarming International Children's Festival takes over. On August 28 the whole place illuminates for Light is Life, a celebration of Šibenik being the first city in the world to have electric street lamps installed (back in 1895). And in September, music conference SHIP Festival is staged at four venues across town. Live music doesn't just extend to the festivals, though. Throughout the year, the theater and nightclub space Tunel

Previous pages, left to right: Šibenik's UNESCO-listed St James Cathedral; Kornati National Park. *Left:* St James' is a beautiful blend of Gothic and Rennaisance architecture. *Below:* Southeast of Šibenik, Dubrovnik is another Dalmation Coast gem.

DON'T LEAVE WITHOUT ...

1. Being wowed by waterfalls: nothing prepares you for the dazzling turquoise green of Krka's Skradinski Buk, where the waters crash over tufa rocks to breathtaking effect.

2. Enjoying fine dining at Michelin-starred Pelegrini, where chef Rudolf Štefan serves four- or six-course tasting menus to lucky patrons, who often number among the country's jet set.

3. Taking a boat trip to the uninhabited islands of nearby Kornati National Park, stopping at lagoons and beaches for swimming, snorkeling and ethereal views.

Below: A quaint alley in Šibenik's Old Town. *Right:* The city lies within easy distance of Krka National Park, a nature-lovers' playground centered around the seven waterfalls (such as superlative Skradinski Buk) of its rushing namesake river.

RatCat hosts DJs and EDM artists, while hill-top citadel St Michael's Fortress doubles up as a concert arena where Air, Róisín Murphy and Röyksopp have recently played.

Petite Šibenik is a perfect microcosm of Croatian culture – but it has to be said, it's the proximity to nature that pulls most first-timers in: many stop over here while visiting the waterfalls of nearby Krka National Park. I was included in that number years ago. My first visit to Šibenik was part of a pilgrimage to Krka, just a 20-minute drive away and, I maintain, the most beautiful park in Croatia. It's got scenic hiking trails, historical sites like Mother of Mercy Monastery on an island in Lake Visovac and, of course, the seven waterfalls – the most famous of which, Skradinski Buk, is utterly magnificent.

Krka is just one of the natural sights close by: there are also estuaries to swim in and pebble beaches like Banj and Rezalište to laze on. If relaxing on Adriatic shores isn't your bag, adrenaline awaits – Zipline Šibenik has three hefty cables installed over Čikola Canyon, which is as thrilling as it sounds. Nature, architecture, dining, festivals, live music – your only conundrum is deciding when to go.

THE NEXT 'IT'
URBAN BEACH DESTINATION

Danang, Vietnam

JAMES PHAM Located roughly in the center of Vietnam, Danang is blessed with mountains, a long city beach and a cool vibe. Add in day-trip options to three UNESCO-listed sites – the tombs and temples of Hue, the Cham temple-towers at My Son, the photogenic town of Hoi An – and there's even more to love.

Danang started appearing on travel 'hot lists' a few years ago and has been building steam ever since, offering something for just about every taste. Nature lovers will gravitate to its forested mountains and long, clean beaches, some conveniently located right in the city center. Foodies will appreciate its up-and-coming dining scene replete with fresh seafood cooked to order, award-winning fine-dining establishments and a plethora of delectable regional specialties. Culture vultures can build multiday itineraries around the world's largest museum dedicated to ancient Cham sculptures, and no less than three UNESCO World Heritage Sites within easy driving distance. And as Danang has an airport with a growing number of direct international flights, as well as being a stop on Vietnam's famed Reunification Express railway (which runs the length of the country), getting in and out couldn't be easier. Affordable housing and the lure of urban comforts combined with a beachside location has enticed many visitors into staying longer than planned.

One of my favorite things to do is to go to the beach at different times of the day. Early mornings, you'll find entire families at the downtown My Khe Beach, getting a swim in before work or school or perhaps joining in a spirited aerobics or dance class somewhere along the boardwalk. However, the beaches practically clear out by 8:30am, leaving sun worshippers all to themselves – until the locals return in the late afternoon.

As a photographer, I love visiting its thriving fish market early in the morning, where fisher-folk drag their circular boats onto the sand and lay out the night's catch for sale. Young locals

Previous pages: Danang is known for its spectacular bridges, but the Golden Bridge is equally stunning, set above the city at Sun World Ba Na Hills theme park. *Above left:* Danang has a host of luxe resorts to choose from. *Above:* Circular fishing boats at Man Thai Beach. *Right:* Early morning fish sellers at Man Thai.

DON'T LEAVE WITHOUT ...

1. Visiting the world's largest collection of ancient Cham artifacts at the Cham Sculpture Museum, showcasing eight centuries of exquisite art.

2. Sampling some of the region's specialties, including crispy *banh xeo* crepes stuffed with shrimp and pork, and fresh seafood cooked to order.

3. Taking a day trip to the ancient royal city of Hue; the atmospheric medieval port town of Hoi An; or the haunting 4th-century Cham temples at My Son.

often turn up with portable stoves and instant noodles, ready to cook up a seafood breakfast that's as fresh as you can get.

But there's so much more than pretty beaches. The picturesque Han River runs parallel to the sea here, so Danang is also known as the 'City of Bridges'. Stretching 2185ft (666m) across the Han, the most iconic of them all is the bright yellow Dragon Bridge, whose arches – complete with steel scales – form the undulating body of a dragon looking towards the sea. At night, it dazzles with colored lights and even breathes water and real fire.

Behind Danang's laid-back vibe, there's a palpable buzz of a destination ready to welcome the world. Michelin added Danang to its guide in 2024; in late 2025, Cirque du Soleil announced a series of large-scale productions to be staged here over the coming years. And between May and July, huge crowds flock in to see the night sky bloom during the Danang International Fireworks Festival. Southeast Asia's largest pyrotechnics event, it features a host of world-class international teams who put on jaw-dropping displays choreographed to music, enhanced by cutting-edge AR technology via smartphone apps. Between pristine natural landscapes, a vibrant culinary scene and an easy-living beach vibe, Danang really *does* have it all.

Far left: Steamed *banh beo* (rice-flour cakes) at a restaurant in Danang's Hai Chau district. *Left:* Ready-to-serve grilled skewers and *banh xeo* crepes stuffed with shrimp and pork at a diner in Danang's Con Market.

BYRON BAY

WITHOUT THE CROWDS

The Tweed, Australia

SARAH REID Famed surf town Byron Bay is only 45 minutes from Gold Coast Airport, but it's the bit in between the two you shouldn't miss. This is the Tweed. The recently launched Tweed Visitor Pledge invites travelers to explore this abundant coastal region with care, curiosity and respect – and there are plenty of new ways to do it.

At the northeastern tip of New South Wales, the Tweed is often described as a more laid-back version of Byron Bay. And it's true – even Byron locals head to this scenic agricultural region to decompress. As one of them, I should know.

I'm a sucker for a lazy weekend spent traipsing between the Tweed's long blond beaches and its lauded coastal restaurants – which include the welcoming Pipit in Pottsville, where chef Ben Devlin's elegant seasonal dishes have bagged an avalanche of awards. But there's more to the Tweed than sand and sustainable seafood.

Rising up behind the coast, the lush green hills of the hinterland – remnants of a massive shield volcano – are bursting with rewarding low-impact activities. The Tweed River snakes down through these hills to regional hub Murwillumbah (Murbah to locals), known for its arts scene and well-preserved art deco buildings erected during the town's dairy boom. One of them houses my favorite local eating option, Bistro Livi, named Regional Restaurant of the Year by the respected *Good Food Guide* in 2024.

Murbah also marks the head of the Northern Rivers Rail Trail, a former rail corridor currently being transformed into an 82-mile (132km) mixed-use pathway. Threading through pockets of emerald rainforest, the first 15-mile (24km) section is ideal for cycling, with bike hire available at Murbah's heritage-listed former train station.

A short hop upriver is the free-spirited town of Uki. It's the gateway to Mt Jerusalem National Park, with a number of ways to immerse yourself in the region's teeming subtropical rainforests. Chief among them is the Gidjuum Gulganyi Walk, a four-day, 26-mile (42km) hiking trail opened in 2025. Meaning 'Old People's Track' in the Bundjalung language of the region's Traditional Custodians, this wild, undulating route

Previous pages: A mist-wreathed sunrise over the Tweed Region's peaks. *Left:* Hiromi Tango's *Rainbow Circles* installation at Murbah's M-Arts Precinct. *Above:* The Tweed River meets mountains and sky in the open country around Murwillumbah.

DON'T LEAVE WITHOUT ...

1. Checking out the Tweed Regional Gallery's latest exhibitions and its unique Margaret Olley Art Centre celebrating the Australian painter's life, career and legacy.

2. Visiting local producers such as Husk Farm Distillery in Tumbulgum, which distills rum from local sugarcane juice; and Farm & Co, which operates a cafe and restaurant on a sunflower and macadamia farm in Cudgen.

3. Experiencing local Aboriginal culture, perhaps on a wild-food-themed Tweed River cruise with Tweed Escapes.

Right: Peak-framed cattle pastures near Murwillumbah. *Above left:* Riverside living along the lush banks of the Tweed in Murbah. *Above right:* Tim Storrier's *The Grand Impedimenta* oversees the grounds at the Tweed Regional Gallery.

linking the Tweed and Byron regions guided me along pathways used by Bundjalung peoples for millennia, with uplifting views aplenty. This wildlife-rich belt of ancient rainforest, crowned by the sacred peak of Wollumbin, has long been a special place for me, but tramping its first multiday trail to a soundtrack of songbirds and endangered frogs forged a deeper connection.

Infrastructure upgrades in the national park also include improved access to Unicorn Falls, which spills into a shaded turquoise pool; and the creation of the Whisky Creek Walk, a meandering 3.3-mile (5.4km) loop along a gin-clear creek. It forms part of the Gidjuum Gulganyi Walk, and for me it was one of the most beautiful sections of the entire route.

Also recently opened is the Uki Mountain Bike Park, with eight trails to explore; fuel up first with an award-winning coffee at Bastion Lane Espresso, housed nearby in Uki's 1909 post office. The Tweed's verdant hills are also dotted with guesthouses within easy reach of the region's natural playgrounds - newcomers include the off-grid architectural glasshouses of Avion Retreat. If you can, align a visit with October's Savour the Tweed festival, when the region unites to celebrate the flavors of this New South Wales idyll on the rise.

LOCAL VIBES, SUGARY BEACHES
AND STUNNING MARINE LIFE

Fulidhoo, Maldives

JAMES PHAM A Maldives getaway inevitably summons up images of what everyone dreams a tropical island paradise should look like. The tiny, easily accessible island of Fulidhoo more than delivers on powdery white sand and limpid waters – but at a fraction of the cost of a typical resort-island stay.

Home to no more than 400 permanent residents, Fulidhoo is one of the Maldives' smallest inhabited islands. Located in the Vaavu Atoll, itself the least populated atoll in this archipelago nation, Fulidhoo measures a scant 2300ft (700m) long by 656ft (200m) wide; it takes just 20 minutes to stroll slowly around the entire island.

For most people, Maldivian vacations conjure images of ultraluxe overwater bungalows on islands completely occupied by a single resort, with eye-watering price tags to match – but Fulidhoo is one of fewer non-resort 100 'local islands' (where Maldivians live) that also have a sprinking of guesthouses. These range from no-frills to boutique-chic, and offer a more budget-friendly but no less enchanting version of tropical paradise. And while the Maldives' nearly 1200 islands are spread across some 34,750 sq miles (90,000 sq km) of ocean, often necessitating an expensive domestic seaplane transfer, Fulidhoo is only about 35 miles (57km) south of the international airport on Malé, and is accessible by a 1½-hour speedboat or 3½-hour ferry ride.

Once I arrived here, it felt as if the outside world had melted away. There was no need for a watch; the melodic calls to prayer were enough to mark the passing of time. I slipped off my shoes and never thought about them again until it was time to leave. The days took on a blissfully mundane routine, starting with a breakfast of *mas huni* – shredded tuna, diced onion and

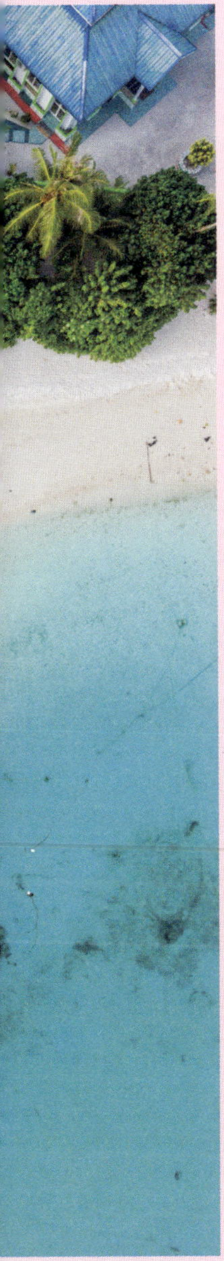

Previous pages: Tiny Fulidhoo is ringed with white-sand beaches and reef-rich waters. *Left:* Chic accommodation at the waterside. *Right:* Stingrays glide near the island's beaches. *Below:* Fulidhoo's mosque sits in quiet, bougainvillea-wreathed backstreets.

grated fresh coconut with a squeeze of lime, all wrapped in a warm *roshi* flatbread.

After breakfast, I headed off to one of the handful of beaches, covered up until I got to one of the designated 'bikini beaches' – a rule observed on local islands like Fulidhoo but not on private resort islands. Life here felt lived rather than curated, with residents heading out to sea to go fishing, gathering for a spirited game of soccer or beach volleyball or simply relaxing in a swing chair.

Another aspect of Fulidhoo's appeal is that sharks and rays swim right up to the island' shores, drawn in by food scraps scattered by fisherfolk and tour operators who arrive in the morning with boatloads of visitors, all in search of that perfect shot. But once the boats leave, it's just you, the sea and the marine life. My favorite time of day was afternoon, spent quietly sitting on the sand, waves lapping at my toes, stingrays and the occasional nurse shark languidly swimming just a few feet away as I pinched myself just to make sure it was real.

Therein lies the beauty of Fulidhoo. There's not much to actually do other than make the rounds of the few casual cafes in town, swim out to the Fulidhoo swing, hit the convenience store for an ice cream, or perhaps go on a day trip to swim with nurse sharks or claim your own deserted sandbank. Once the sun sets, the options are even fewer: curl up with a book or round up a few friends for board games, in the blissful knowledge that you can do it all again the next day.

Left main: Shoreside palms. *Left inset:* Rays swim right up to the shore on Fulidhoo, making for easy-access marine encounters. *Above:* A bird's-eye view over Fulidhoo's slim strip of land.

DON'T LEAVE WITHOUT ...

1. Taking the time to walk around the perimeter of the island, visiting local and bikini beaches and soaking up the chill barefoot atmosphere.

2. Swimming out to the Fulidhoo swing, set in the sea about 328ft (100m) offshore; you might even see dolphins in the distance.

3. Embark on a boat excursion to Shark Point, swimming with nurse sharks and manta rays and stopping off at a deserted sandbank.

NICARAGUA'S ENDURING FAIRY-TALE CITY

Granada, Nicaragua

ROBERT ISENBERG Combined with nearby natural wonders, this charming city's well-preserved beauty showcases some of Nicaragua's proudest qualities. After centuries of triumph and tragedy, Granada now reigns as the nation's most coveted destination.

Dancers swayed and whirled in the Plaza Mayor, their crimson dresses flaring in perfect synchronicity. Men in Cordovan hats stepped lithely around their partners, and the sultry air throbbed with amplified folk songs. The noise and music would have enthralled me anywhere, yet the setting made it all the better: crowds clapped along, Christmas lights crisscrossed the square and the bright yellow walls of the Catedral de Granada rose regally above.

I hadn't planned to visit Granada during La Purísima, a December religious festival that celebrates the Virgin Mary. The miraculous timing meant night after night of street parties, fantastic food stands and fireworks displays that lit up the cathedral's famous scarlet dome. Yet I also knew that Granada needs no special occasion to cast its spell on visitors. The city – which celebrated its quincentennial in 2024 – feels frozen in its 19th-century grandeur: ranks of Spanish Viceregal buildings line the streets, painted in the jaunty colors of a bygone era. Wooden doors open onto ornate tiled walkways and verdant courtyards. Walls are decked with handsome balconies and antique-looking lamps. On the hazy horizon, you'll spot the slouched profile of mythic volcano Mombacho.

It's hard to believe that US soldier-of-fortune William Walker torched Granada to the ground in 1856, after which the city had to be rebuilt from rubble. Today, horse-drawn carriages and handmade ceramic street signs would have you believe Granada has looked this splendid since its genesis. Historic row houses now hold high-end restaurants and luxury hotels, and a parade of churches represent a range of architectural styles. Even the occasional ruin is magnificent: the crumbling brickwork of the Antiguo Hospital is a favorite subject for photographers.

Keep walking east and you'll meet the sandy shores of Lago de Nicaragua (aka Lago Cocibolca), Central America's

Previous pages: Bold colors dominate Granada's picturesque streetscapes. *Left:* Pedestrianized Calle la Calzada, lined with cafes, restaurants and souvenir stalls. *Below:* Farm-fresh local produce along Calle el Comercio (Market St).

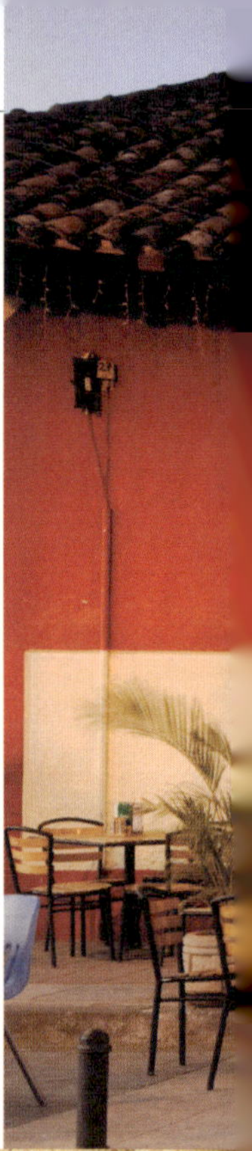

DON'T LEAVE WITHOUT ...

1. Spending an evening in the Plaza Mayor; this central park comes alive at night, drawing locals and tourists alike, and the plaza is ringed with restaurants.

2. Checking out the chocolatiers: two neighboring institutions, the ChocoMuseo and the Argencove Chocolate Factory, are fierce competitors – and both offer masterful tours and gifts.

3. Strolling the esplanade along Lago de Nicaragua, enjoying lakeside views and cocktails at the beachfront bars just southeast of town.

Below left: Grand Spanish Viceregal facades along Calle la Calzada. *Below:* Vibrant hammocks. *Right:* Early evening drinks along Calle la Calzada.

largest freshwater lake. One of my most cherished memories is paddling kayaks with my friend Bill into Las Isletas, a maze of 365 tiny islands with narrow channels in between. Indigenous Nicaraguans and modern scientists actually agree on its origins: millennia ago, in a moment of seismic fury, Mombacho exploded, launching colossal boulders into the air. These hunks of rock cooled and, over time, accumulated topsoil and plant life. Floating down murky canals and slicing through tangled lilies, we spotted half-hidden cottages, fisherfolk casting nets and monkeys fidgeting in trees.

Some of my most memorable times in Granada have centered around the conversations I've enjoyed with locals. I talked long into the night with Yexira, the owner of my hotel; shared many bottles of Toña beer with Amós Abdias, the owner and chef at acclaimed local eatery Tostometro; and chatted about stogies at iconic cigar-maker Doña Elba. The people of Granada are proud of their city, which has bounced back from so much misfortune. Viva Granada, I thought. May it still stand in 500 more years.

SMALL-TOWN GERMANY, BIG-DESIGN IDEAS

Dessau, Germany

ANTHONY HAM One hundred years ago, Bauhaus came to the charming small town of Dessau – or Dessau-Rosslau, to give it its proper name – in Berlin's hinterland. It's difficult to overstate the importance of that moment. Bauhaus is the biggest of all design ideas, one that still goes to the heart of our everyday lives a century later.

Although founded in Weimar in 1919, it was in Dessau that Bauhaus became the life-changing design principle that we know today. The idea behind Bauhaus is simple: less is more. It may not sound like such a radical concept, but once Bauhaus took hold, design shifted from an aesthetic indulgence to something that could make people's lives better.

In his book *Bauhaus*, Frank Whitford described its influence thus: 'Everyone sitting on a chair with a tubular steel frame, using an adjustable reading lamp or living in a house partly or entirely constructed from prefabricated elements is benefiting from a revolution…largely brought about by the Bauhaus.'

So why is Dessau a design icon? Unlike many small industrial towns in the central German heartland, the city's authorities had the vision to imagine a very different way forward, and lured the Bauhaus founders here in the 1920s. They began by building the Bauhausgebäude (Bauhaus Building); it's still a design school but is partially open to the public. Always my first Dessau stop, this box-like structure – the Bauhaus Ground Zero – is true to Bauhaus principles: it's more brilliant than beautiful.

So widespread is the influence of Bauhaus design on modern Dessau that, on my first visit, it was easy to miss the references. And then, all of a sudden, I saw it everywhere and found myself nodding in recognition. The genius of Bauhaus is that it more closely resembles real life than design. The sheer functionality of the Bauhaus concept means that visiting Dessau feels like going to the source of how we interact with the architecture of our daily lives. So with that in mind, I always head south of the center for a taste of Bauhaus at its most prosaic, taking

Previous pages: Walter Gropius' iconic Bauhausgebäude (Bauhaus Building). *Above left:* Don't miss dinner at Kornhaus, set in an Elbe-facing building designed by Gropius' assistant Carl Flieger. *Above:* Dessau's cityscape blends the old and the new. *Right:* Function rather than form dictated the Bauhaus Building's design.

DON'T LEAVE WITHOUT ...

1. Strolling the banks of the River Elbe, admiring the Old Town's baroque skyline, with Dessau on one riverbank, Rosslau on the other.

2. Diving into Dessau's cobbled historic core, visiting palaces, public squares and a cathedral – a necessary extravagance to offset the relentless functionality of the Bauhaus oeuvre.

3. Booking dinner at Kornhaus, set by the side of the Elbe; this standout Bauhaus-inspired beer-and-meals hall was designed by Carl Flieger, an assistant to Walter Gropius.

Tram No 1 to the Siedlung Törten. This 1920s-era working-class estate comprises more than 300 Bauhaus-inspired homes, and if ever the power of Bauhaus as an idea to improve the lives of ordinary people was on show, it's here. The houses are brilliant in their square-angled ordinariness, in their departure from the ornamental flourishes that define the pre-Bauhaus architecture of Dessau's older quarters.

Back in town, my next stop is the Meisterhäuser, the homes of Bauhaus' leading lights – from the movement's founder Walter Gropius to painters Wassily Kandinsky and Paul Klee. These cubist buildings reimagined the use of interior space, and though their designs were radical in the 1930s, they're now considered the forerunners to modern homes. But sometimes here, I feel like I'm a witness to design experiments that didn't stand the test of time – like the low balcony rails at Haus Muche/Schlemmer, which would never pass modern safety standards.

As a school of design, Bauhaus only survived a mere 15 years, interrupted by WWII and a world eager to break with the ideas of the past. But the influence of Bauhaus lived (and lives) on. Thanks to Dessau.

Far left: Prosaically known as The Eierschneider (the Egg slicer), the graceful Tiergartenbrücke spans the Elbe on Dessau's eastern side. *Left:* Clean Bauhaus lines shine at pub-restaurant Kornhaus.

MAGICAL LANDSCAPES
OF FICTION AND FORAGING

Prince Edward Island, Canada

CAROLINE TREFLER Prince Edward Island (PEI) is Canada's smallest province but the allure is giant. Lighthouses, white-sand beaches, red sandstone cliffs and rolling green hills beckon you to explore by car, by bike or on foot. And its nickname – 'Canada's Food Island' – makes it clear you'll eat well everywhere you go.

I'm Canadian and I grew up in a family of redheads. If you're familiar with *Anne of Green Gables*, you'll have an inkling of what this meant to my childhood: before I understood the concept of 'travel', I knew that PEI was magical. While some come here for the scenery and the food, others because of Anne, the fictional red-haired orphan created by Lucy Maud Montgomery.

Anne of Green Gables has been translated into more than 35 languages and sold over 50 million copies. It's been turned into movies, TV series, plays and musicals. Anne is so compelling because she isn't just feisty, she's also a dreamer and a storyteller who can bestow a gleam of beauty and a glint of mystery on everything and everyone around her. I think a lot of kids identify with her, but I felt a special kinship – I was about 10 when my carrot-orange-haired aunt gave me a hard-cover copy of *Anne of Green Gables*. I always used to read my favorite books over and over, but this one was different, almost a totem.

In PEI you can visit Green Gables Heritage Place (inspiration for the fictional Green Gables), where you can gaze into the Enchanted Bookcase, walk the Haunted Wood and Lovers Lane and gaze over the Lake of Shining Waters. The Anne of Green Gables Museum, in a farmhouse built by Montgomery's aunt and uncle, is furnished with many of the author's belongings.

And there are so many more ways to find magic in PEI. When I finally visited, I biked part of the 279-mile-long (449km) Confederation Trail, which runs from one tip of the island to the other. I walked the floating boardwalk of Greenwich National Park and went barefoot on the beach. I soaked in the thermal waters and ever-so-briefly ducked into the cold plunge pool at Mysa Nordic Spa. I ate PEI oysters, blueberries, potatoes, lobster rolls and freshly grilled

Previous pages, left to right: Wood Islands Lighthouse, on PEI's southeastern shore; Snow-crab pots. *Left:* Fresh seafood is a menu staple at PEI's welcoming restaurants. *Above:* Shoreside color at North Rustico Harbour.

DON'T LEAVE WITHOUT ...

1. Attending the Fireworks Feast at Inn at Bay Fortune: it starts with oysters and fire-roasted hors d'oeuvres in the garden, followed by a spectacular sit-down meal by the giant hearth.

2. Taking a twilight soak at Mysa Nordic Spa, followed by dinner at the guest-only restaurant.

3. Spending Saturday morning at the year-round Charlottetown Farmers Market, looking for artisanal crafts and great food to eat and take home as souvenirs.

Right: Ready to shuck during the 'Oyster Hour' bivalve bonanza at the Inn at Bay Fortune. *Above left:* Fishing huts and boats line the pier at pretty Stanley Bridge. *Above right:* Rugged coastal dunes.

mackerel that I caught myself. And I met so many storytellers.

In Georgetown, Peter Llewelyn, owner of the custom jewelry shop Shoreline Design and once the town's mayor, regaled us with tales of his life as he walked us around his neighborhood. We had to tear ourselves away from Therese, the self-described caretaker of Mair Family Museum – 'Open by chance' says a sign out front – who imparted generations of stories about her family, the source of the museum's prolific display of belongings. Out on the water, Perry Gotell, owner and operator of Tranquility Cove Adventures, bewitched us with accounts of lobster trapping, crab harvesting and mussel cultivating. At the Inn at Bay Fortune, farmer Kevin Petrie charmed a crowd as he explained sustainable farming practices; the restaurant's resident chef-forager, Nick Chindamo, treated us to a walking education about the island's edible plants and sea vegetables. As he picked bits of this and that for us to smell or taste, I wrote in my notebook that I was learning to see the landscape like a salad.

It's a small island, but it inspires a lot of stories.

SOFT SHELLS AND A HEART OF GOLD

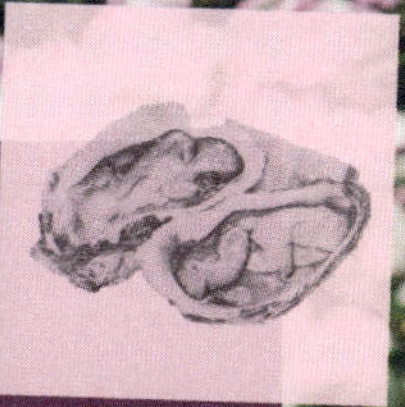

Maryland, USA

JULIE F KING Maryland is my adopted hometown, a place I love beyond measure or reason. I delight in its lush rolling hills, diverse coastal playgrounds, local quirkiness, maritime history and, of course, its array of fresh seafood. Take it from me: Maryland will draw you in and keep you coming back for more.

Since I arrived in Maryland almost 20 years ago as a medical student, I've become a true Marylander – loyal to the Orioles and Ravens, proud of our heritage as home to Harriet Tubman's Underground Railroad, Frederick Douglass, Tupac Shakur and Oprah Winfrey. It's a cultural powerhouse, a culinary destination and an outdoor paradise.

The state's awesomeness is blatantly obvious in Annapolis, the USA's first peacetime capital. Here, John Adams and Benjamin Franklin signed the Treaty of Paris in 1783, thus ending the Revolutionary War; today, it's the state capital and home to the prestigious Naval Academy. Wander to the 'Republic of Eastport', where Davis' Pub has its roots in Annapolis' 19th-century maritime history. Its eponymous original owner, George Washington Davis, was a Black entrepreneur who, in the early 1900s, transformed this former sweet shop into a bar for the neighborhood's Black watermen.

Move on south over the Bay Bridge, towards the Eastern Shore and down Rte 50 (the 'Ocean Gateway') for a taste of boardwalk kitsch, fries and soft-serve in Ocean City; or seek solace on the Assateague National Seashore, a 37-mile-long (60km) barrier island where wild horses and shorebirds roam. At inland Sharpsburg in Western Maryland, I like to engage my inner Civil War history buff at the Antietam National Battlefield's Pry Barn, which served as Union commander General McClellan's outpost during the conflict and as a temporary field hospital. There's more history in nearby Frederick, a stop

Previous pages, left to right: Chesapeake City from Chesapeake City Bridge; Spring blooms. Left: Row houses in Federal Hill, Baltimore. Right: Antique cannon at Baltimore's Fort McHenry. Below: Wild horses roam free on Assateague Island National Seashore.

Orioles
STORE
O'NEILL
21

on the B&O (Baltimore and Ohio) Railroad – the USA's oldest (founded 1827). I usually grab dinner at Frederick's Wye Oak Tavern, where the Voltaggio brothers pay homage to the art of the gathering space in their hometown.

Baltimore is a classic case of 'To know it, is to love it'. Our bumper stickers say it best: 'Baltimore: actually, I like it'. During baseball season, an Orioles game at Camden Yards is a must. There's no bad seat in the house, but my preferred spot is section 336 on the upper deck – an unparalleled vantage point from which to take in the gorgeous field, the former *Baltimore Sun* clock on the horizon and the old B&O Warehouse in relief.

Head east through the Inner Harbor, where our famed National Aquarium overlooks the water, and continue east through the cobblestone streets of historic Fells Point. Get inspired by the art of coastal design at home goods store Su Casa, marvel at the beauty and breadth of pastry options at Sacré Sucré, and savor local bivalves at Thames Street Oyster House. But if you only eat one meal, let it be at Peter's Inn. Sit at the bar and get the 'martini service': a brimming coupe with all the accoutrements, plus a second 'sidecar' serving. Their iconic garlic bread will change your life. And if you're lucky, you may even get to chat with the owners, Bud and Karin Tiffany, whose banter and gracious hosting evoke the ideal of hospitality. After all, Maryland's finest asset is its profoundly proud and friendly people, who are always ready to welcome guests.

Left main: Baltimore's Inner Harbor waterfront. *Left inset:* Game day cowds on Eutaw St, near the Camden Yards ball park in Baltimore. *Above:* The classic Maryland crab cake has golden breadcrumbs, chunky crab flakes and Old Bay seasoning.

DON'T LEAVE WITHOUT ...

1. Sampling Baltimore's delicious specialty: crab cakes. My favorites are at Pappas, Faidley's and Koco's.

2. Spending at least one night at one of Maryland's grande-dame hotels – Inn at Perry Cabin in St Michaels is sublime; Baltimore's Ivy Hotel is a slice of heaven.

3. Getting out on the Chesapeake Bay: take a schooner tour, rent a kayak in one of the state's parks, or try a 'hook and cook' fishing experience.

MOUNTAINSIDE ADVENTURES AND OPEN-WATER SWIMMING

Bariloche and the Lakes District, Argentina

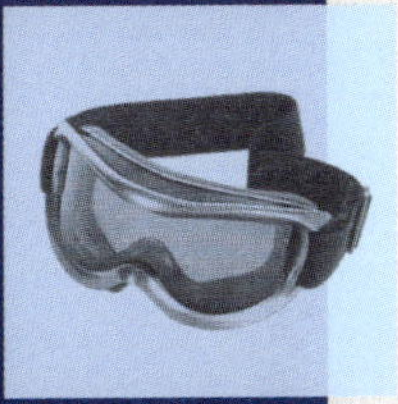

CHRISTINE GILBERT San Carlos de Bariloche is a place that will hold you – not in restraint, but in care. Known as the 'Gateway to Patagonia', this good-looking adventure hub is the gateway to Argentina's Lake District, a region replete with natural bodies of water, mountains and a bit of mystery.

To me, Bariloche feels more like a Swiss town ensconced in the forests of the Andes than a city of nearly 136,000 people. Bordering Lago Nahuel Huapi – the Lake District's largest and deepest lake – Bariloche is walkable though hilly, giving plenty of practice for mountain trekking in the surrounding Parque Nacional Nahuel Huapi.

Close to the national park entrance at Villa Los Cohiues lie the trailheads for three of my favorite hikes: the 10-minute stroll to the rushing waters of Cascada de los Duendes; the hour-long round trip to Mirador Lago Gutiérrez, with its heady Lake District views; and the four-hour trek to Refugio Frey. This rustic mountain lodge sits on the shores of Laguna Toncek, and after the hike here, I like refreshing my feet by dipping them into Toncek's icy waters, then reenergizing with a bowl of the *refugio's* delicious lentil stew.

Frey is the first of four *refugios* along the 28.5-mile (46km) hut-to-hut trek traversing the national park, which can be hiked in four days if the weather allows – pre-booking accommodation is required (you can do so at the national park office in town, or via the website). The *refugio* is also a base for over 100 traditional and sport rock-climbing routes zig-zagging up the surrounding granite spires; you'll need to either bring your own gear and – ideally – a climbing guide-book, or pre-book a guide and gear rental with local outfits such as Entropia Escalada.

When not scaling the Andes, I like to get in the (chilly) water. Renting a car, taking the bus or even hitchhiking (most everyone here does) around town gives me access to plenty of lakes for swimming. Along the shores of Lago Nahuel Huapi, Playas Bonita and Serena offer ample amenities and even lifeguard services; Lago Gutiérrez has warmer waters and is a popular stop for cyclists. However, any lake you find your-self by is usually the best option. While the only predators

Previous pages: The pointed peaks of Cerro Catedral, high above Bariloche. *Left:* Luxe lakeside retreat Llao Llao Hotel enjoys superlative views of Lago Nahuel Huapi. *Below:* Skiers scoot up to the Cerro Catedral slopes by chairlift from Bariloche.

DON'T LEAVE WITHOUT ...

1. Driving the incredbile 68-mile (110km) Ruta de Siete Lagos (Route of the Seven Lakes) between Villa La Angostura and San Martín de los Andes.

2. Taking the chairlift up Cerro Campanario to take in 360-degree views of Lago Nahuel Huapi, Cerro Catedral ski area and the Llao Llao Hotel, a luxury lakeside resort that's hosted foreign dignitaries.

3. Sampling Ãnima Restaurante's locally sourced, inventive menu, paired with Argentine wines and served in a whimsical tree-nestled salon.

Below left: Sip hot chocolate or shop for artisan cacao confections at the parade of stores lining Calle Mitre in central Bariloche. *Below:* The reward for a four-hour uphill trek from Bariloche, rustic Refugio Frey sits on the shores of Laguna Toncek. *Right:* The city's neo-Gothic Catedral Nuestra Señora del Nahuel Huapi.

in the area are pumas (which usually keep to themselves), do keep eyes peeled for Nahuelito, a dinosaur-like water monster said to live in Nahuel Huapi's depths.

After a long trek, climb or cold-water swim, it's time to head to Bariloche's main street, Calle Mitre, to sip hot chocolate and eat waffles piled high with Chantilly cream at Rapanui, a wonderland rivaling Willy Wonka's chocolate factory. Mitre is lined with chocolate shops, but Rapanui is the only one with its own ice-skating rink, and it has the most decadent chocolate selection in town – you can select your own truffles for a customized boxed set.

On the way home, I make the trip to the airport via Ruta 40. Just before Calle Rivadavia, there's a large roadside shrine of red banners and small statues that's dedicated to the popular saint of travelers, Gauchito. It's customary for Argentine truckers to ask the Gauchito for protection to reach their destination. You can do the same – but should you reach home safely, you must return one day to leave him a token of your appreciation.

LA DOLCE VITA

IN A SINGLE ITALIAN REGION

Veneto, Italy

JULIA BUCKLEY This northeastern region of Italy attracts visitors to Venice, but few venture into the wider area. Yet Veneto is Italy in microcosm, with spectacular natural landscapes from the Dolomites to Lake Garda, sublime Renaissance cities including Verona and Padua – and some of Italy's best food and wine, from Prosecco and the legendary tiramisu.

Take medieval cities and Renaissance art. Add mountains, beaches, one of Europe's greatest lakes – and blend with world-class food and wine. Italy? *Ma certo*, but specifically Veneto. This northeastern region brings together the best of the *Bel Paese* (Beautiful Country), but it often gets overlooked in the hyperfocus on its capital, Venice. After all, what could compete with La Serenissima?

Well, Padua (Padova in Italian) for starters. You could argue that the Renaissance actually began here in 1305, when artist Giotto began decorating a chapel for local loan shark Enrico Scrovegni. Giotto was already a celebrity, but his frescoes in the Scrovegni Chapel were something else – his scenes from the life of Jesus and the Virgin Mary are some of the first depictions of human emotion in art history. It was here, under Giotto's blue sky and twinkly-starred roof, that I first fell in love with painting. It was as if the walls could speak.

That's the wonderful thing about Veneto – while Venice's staggering beauty can be overwhelming (even for someone like me, who lives there), the wider area is a regular, modern region studded with memory vaults from the past. Padua's medieval porticoes are a delight; Vicenza's main drag, Corso Palladio, is a catwalk of Renaissance mansions, built over the original Roman street. In Verona, that Roman heritage is still proudly on display – the pink-stone amphitheater is said to be the best preserved in the world.

The smaller towns are a joy, too: coastal Chioggia is a mini Venice; canals also wreath the elegant Renaissance center of inland Treviso. Bassano has its Ponte Vecchio, a wooden bridge over the Brenta River designed by Renaissance

Previous pages: Verona's ancient Roman amphitheater. *Above left:* Hike the spectacular Dolomites in northern Veneto. *Above:* Palladio's dramatic Teatro Olimpico in UNESCO-listed Vicenza. *Right:* The core of Vicenza's Palazzo da Schio Ca' d'Oro dates back to the 14th century.

DON'T LEAVE WITHOUT ...

1. Catching a concert at Vicenza's Teatro Olimpico. The oldest masonry-built theater in the world was designed by Palladio – and still hosts regular performances.

2. Sailing into Lombardy. Lake Garda straddles both regions, and a ferry to Sirmione will punt you across the border and back in time, to medieval and Roman remains.

3. Trying authentic tiramisu. Italy's beloved dessert is said to have been invented at Le Beccherie in Treviso, as a pick-me-up for pregnant owner Alba Campeol.

'starchitect' Andrea Palladio. A Vicenza native, he dotted Veneto's rollercoaster Euganean Hills with sumptuous mansions; my favorite, Villa La Rotonda, was the inspiration for the White House.

You want the great outdoors? Head north to that other UNESCO World Heritage Site, the Dolomites (perhaps stopping en route in the UNESCO-protected Prosecco Hills, for a flight of the world's most popular sparkling wine). But life in these pink-tinged mountains isn't all skiing and hiking – this is also road-trip country, where you can spend the morning in the clouds at the Messner Mountain Museum Dolomites (altitude: 7155ft/2180m) and then shuffle down to feast on Alpine delicacies at El Brite de Larieto, a Michelin-recommended *agriturismo* outside Cortina.

For *dolce far niente,* Italy's signature lazy living, the peninsula straddling Venice's lagoon and the Adriatic has shin-deep golden sands from Punta Sabbioni to Jesolo, while west of Verona is glistening Garda, Italy's largest lake. Whisk across the water on ferries, race around the shoreline as 007 did in *Quantum of Solace*, or head into the hills to try the region's other blockbuster wines, Valpolicella and Amarone – they go down a treat swirled into risotto. This is *dolce vita*, Veneto style. Why would you go anywhere else?

Far left: Cruise Lake Garda into Lombardy, where shore-side Sirmione is home to Castello Scaligero. *Left:* The Reinhold Messner Museum in Plan de Corones.

A SOPHISTICATED, SLOW-PACED 'HAPPY CITY'

Chengdu, China

PIERA CHEN There's a Chinese saying, 'Don't go to Sichuan when you're young' – meaning the easy life will dull ambition. *Joie de vivre*, traditionally associated with Sichuan, is epitomized by Chengdu, the provincial capital and China's most inclusive city. From tea to hip-hop, Chengduers make an art of their lives – and welcome you to do the same.

Chengdu's food scene has it all, whether you're after carp in fiery broth, nutty *dandan* noodles or a plate of beautifully blistered dry-fried string beans. This epicurean heaven is the cradle of Sichuan cuisine, and was one of the first mainland Chinese cities deemed worthy of its own Michelin guide.

I usually start my day here with a stuffed *guo hui* flatbread; lunch could be a *prix fixe* menu of elevated classics such as spicy *mapo* tofu and cold rabbit. For dinner, I might curate my own skewer bouquet at a roadside *chuan chuan* stall and watch it sizzle while I wait. At popular hole-in-the-wall spots, it's common to see people across the social classes sharing tables – Chengduers are wise, especially when it comes to enjoying life.

This enjoyment is also palpable in the capital's teahouses, with their stackable bamboo chairs, swan-necked copper kettles and waiters on standby. Teahouses are set in the city's historic temples and parks these days, but before the urban renewal of the mid-1990s, every alley had one – where elders hung out, playing mahjong and minding grandchildren who would grow up drinking tea. I've been told this is why, come 3pm on a sunny day, gens A to Z turn up at Chengdu's teahouses today.

And as the center of the ancient Shu kingdom (2000–1100 BCE), which gave the world stupendous Bronze Age relics, Chengdu has plenty of more formal culture to discover. At the Sanxingdui Museum in nearby Guanghan, I was riveted by fantastical artifacts that some archaeologists consider more historically important than Xi'an's Terracotta Warriors – huge masks evoking extraterrestrials, and tall bronze trees decked with veined leaves and strange fowl. For masks of a different kind, I head to Jinjiang Theater. It specializes in Sichuan opera and its crowd-pleasing

Previous pages: Chengduers grow up drinking tea, and the city's teahouses – set across its parks and temples – are enduringly popular across the generations. *Left:* A waiter prepares tea at one of Chengdu's historic teahouses.

DON'T LEAVE WITHOUT ...

1. Visiting Pengzhen Old Town to have tea: try China's oldest surviving teahouse, Guanyin Pavilion; or Yongfeng Tea Society, converted from a Cultural Revolution–era ironworks.

2. Trying a *mala* dish at Yongle Restaurant; '*ma*' refers to the tingly effects of Sichuan peppercorns, '*la*' to the hotness of chilies (beware: it's addictive).

3. Wandering around Yulin to enjoy its engaging symbiosis of old and new, stopping off at Yulin Comprehensive Market and at queer-friendly bars and cafes.

Right: Venture from Chengdu's center to marvelous museums and ancient towns such as Hakka settlement Luodai. *Above left:* Sitting down to a sizzling beef hotpot at one of Chengdu's renowned restaurants. *Above right:* Freshly fried crayfish, ready to serve..

subgenre, face-changing – the instantaneous changing of masks by performers, using techniques once regarded as state secrets. Also well-guarded is the giant panda, native to Sichuan; you can meet China's vulnerable bamboo-munching mascots at the Giant Panda Breeding Research Centre, just north of the city center.

Unofficially, Chengdu is China's 'queer capital', with a relatively visible LGBTIQ+ culture. I never tire of hanging out in the sycamore-lined neighborhood of Yulin, known for its young-artist community and inclusive vibe; Mintone Records, with its bar/cafe, is a great place to delve into the scene. Chengdu is also China's number one hip-hop city – the biting Sichuan dialect lends itself well to rap, as you'll see if you hit up PH Club and 工Gong; and in April, indie artists from all over China perform at Chengdu's ChunYou Music Festival.

There's also plenty to do outdoors. This bike-friendly place is home to the 62-mile (100km) Tianfu Greenway, the country's longest cycle path, which winds a scenic route through parks, cultural landmarks, riversides and into the foothills; it's popular with all kinds of riders, from Spandex-clad pros to students.

A city of spice and everything nice, Chengdu is a place where you can live richly without breaking the bank.

THIS FAR SOUTH,
THINGS START TO GET A LITTLE WEIRD

Dunedin & the Waitaki, New Zealand

JESSICA LOCKHART Once considered the 'Edinburgh of the South', Dunedin has finally shaken off its European heritage to carve out its own identity. Combine it with a visit to neighboring Ōamaru and you'll find yourself in one of New Zealand's coolest and quirkiest corners.

On an unassuming street in Dunedin – not far from the University of Otago – sits a Victorian villa housing a museum unlike any other. Rap on the door with the crab knocker and you'll be admitted by curator Bruce Mahalski, a visual artist who is best known for his ornate bone sculptures. ('I AM ACTUALLY VERY FRIENDLY!' reads a placard on his desk.)

The Museum of Natural Mystery tells the story of Dunedin via an unusual collection of scientific oddities, cultural objects and ephemera. A two-headed calf sits below a kinetic parrot sculpture. A mummified cat stretches out on the wall. The bones of a long-ago extinct moa, paranormal research books and framed WWII propaganda are also on display.

It's a spot that could only ever exist in Dunedin, which has emerged as one of New Zealand/Aotearoa's most idiosyncratic destinations. Once celebrated for its Scottish heritage – a legacy that's still visible in its Victorian architecture and love of blood sausage – Dunedin is now that impossibly cool guy who lives on the second floor in your building. Yes, he has a dark sense of humor and immaculate taste in food, art and music, but – like Mahalski – he's actually very friendly.

This unique identity first started forming 200 years ago, when Scottish immigrants, gold prospectors and iconoclastic entrepreneurs set up shop on Dunedin's shores. Today, the city's relative isolation and thriving student scene (they account for 20% of the population) have both contributed to its willingness (and need)

Previous pages: Sheep grazing in Sandfly Bay, Dunedin. *Left:* Inside the Grainstore Gallery in Ōamaru's Victorian Precinct. *Right:* Vibrant Dunedin has a big student population. *Below:* A mural of a tuatara by ROA brings Aotearoa wildlife to Bath St in Dunedin.

to do things differently. It's where you'll find NZ's only castle (Lanarch); a secluded cove that's only accessible via a hand-carved tunnel through the rock (Tunnel Beach); and whisky made from bread that would have otherwise gone to landfill (at Dunedin Craft Distillers).

Ninety minutes north is the Waitaki's Ōamaru. Like its bigger sibling, the town is known for its Victorian architecture, which innovative locals saw as the perfect staging ground for steampunk culture. The science fiction genre took off here when the region's farmers started transforming farmyard scraps into interactive sculptures. At Steampunk HQ, you can see steam whistle from a giant zephyr, hear the grinding of a doomsday clock or climb inside a train car that doubles as a movie theater.

Both Dunedin and Ōamaru are full of characters. Under the shade of flowering rātā trees, Gregor Campbell, owner of Tales from Darkest Dunedin, takes me on a guided tour of a cemetary, sharing stories of Chinese gold prospectors and Māori who fought during the Land Wars. On its surface, a graveyard tour sounds macabre, but not the way Campbell tells it: 'I think cemeteries are like libraries, but they're also places of great love – and with great love comes great loss and great sorrow.'

It's a tour you might only find in Dunedin.

Left: Wildflower-speckled sea cliffs near Dunedin. *Above:* Otago's coastline offers spectacular vistas and ample opportunities for spotting Aotearoa's unique birdlife.

DON'T LEAVE WITHOUT ...

1. Spotting NZ's rare endemic birds on Otago's shoreline, such as hoiho at the OPERA reserve, toroa at Pukekura/Taiaroa Head, and colorful takahē at Orokonui Sanctuary en route to Ōamaru.

2. Wandering through geological oddities at Waitaki Whitestone Geopark – including Moeraki's perfectly spherical beach boulders, and Duntroon's elephant-like karst limestone structures.

3. Exploring filming locations like Dunedin's railway station and Ōamaru's Victorian Precinct.

SAVOR THIS ANCIENT CITY'S TIMELESS CHARM

León, Spain

MARK EVELEIGH With a strategic position that dominates the Castilla y León Meseta, León is one of Spain's most evocative and fascinating medieval cities. Dating back to Roman times, it has long been an important spot for traders, mercenaries, knights and pilgrims – and yet these days it's blissfully off the tourist radar.

I've visited León several times, but I never caught a real sense of the city's historical significance until I shuffled in after 300 footsore miles (483km) of hiking the Camino Francés (part of the Camino de Santiago pilgrimage route) from the French border. Perhaps walking the seemingly limitless Spanish steppes – frequently traipsing along arrow-straight tracks laid out by Roman engineers – had sharpened my anticipation. When I finally shambled into León's Casco Antiguo (Old Town) it was with an appropriate sense of awe, coupled with immense gratitude.

I stared up at the spires of the medieval cathedral with the sort of spellbound wonderment that a medieval peasant might have felt at their first glimpse of one of the Iberian Peninsula's greatest monuments. Known locally as Casa de la Luz (House of Light) for its 130 stained-glass windows, the cathedral is just one of León's many historical treasures. Within five minutes' walk you find Parque del Cid, dedicated to the Castilian knight (actually more of a 'sword-for-hire' mercenary) who is Spain's greatest historical hero. The neighboring Basílica de San Isidoro houses what some historians claim was the original Holy Grail, the chalice that Jesus used at the Last Supper. It was transported here from Jerusalem 900 years ago as a simple onyx goblet, and later adorned with the gold and jewels that you see today.

But the city's roots date back much further: León was known to the Romans as Legio (Camp of the Legion). San Isidoro was built on the ruins of a temple to Mercury, and the cathedral was constructed over ancient baths. Even before the building was largely completed (in 1302), the workers realized they had a serious problem with rising damp. Could it have been an inside joke on the part of the local sculptors to decorate the facade with bizarre human faces that have foliage sprouting from their mouths? Some historians say that

Previous pages, left to right: León's soaring 13th-century cathedral, aka Casa de la Luz (House of Light); inside the Basílica de San Isidoro. *Left:* Outdoor dining in Barrio Húmedo. *Below:* Pilgrims hike the ancient Camino Francés trail to León.

DON'T LEAVE WITHOUT ...

1. Visiting the cathedral – in fact, go more than once since, as thanks to the vast areas of stained-glass windows, the illumination changes spectacularly throughout the day.

2. Checking out the city's traditional markets: head to Plaza Mayor on Wednesdays and Saturdays, or Mercado del Conde Luna (open every day apart from Sunday).

3. Sampling León's meaty specialties, from *cecina* (dry-cured beef) and *morcilla de León* (herby pigs' blood sausages) to *lechazo* (suckling goat slow-roasted in a wood-fired oven).

Below left: At the eastern end of León's Old Town, time-worn Plaza Mayor hosts a busy twice-weekly produce market. *Below:* Romanesque San Isidoro dates back to 1063. *Right:* León's Basílica de San Isidoro is said to house the original Holy Grail.

these *hombres verdes* (green men) might date back to ancient Iberian tribal beliefs that predate even the Romans.

Despite its location amid the sunbaked plains of northern Spain, León has recently gained an enviable reputation for 'humidity' thanks to the popularity of the lively San Martín district – known to locals as the Barrio Húmedo (Damp Quarter) for its profusion of bars. It was this, as much as the city's historical wealth, that had enticed this thirsty pilgrim into the Old Town. After three weeks of dorms and simple *menú del día* (daily menu) sustenance, I gratefully dropped my backpack in a pastel-painted room in the 18th-century Hostal San Martín and made my way down to the neighborhood, now one of northern Spain's most appealing nocturnal hangouts. After the long hike through sleepy villages, the crowded bars – clamorous with the clink of glasses, the rattle of tapas saucers and bellows of Spanish laughter – were as welcoming as a warm bath.

Whether you pass fleetingly through as a pilgrim or take time to get to know León more intimately, it doesn't take long to unearth the appeal of Spain's friendliest medieval city.

Bocas del Toro, Panama

ROBERT ISENBERG Slow-paced but well developed, Panama's out-of-the-way archipelago is a longtime hangout for backpackers making their way around Central America. This is a prime location to chill out and work on your tan, for sure – but there's plenty to discover away from the beaches and hammocks: watersports, wildlife-spotting and an inspired culinary scene.

Through my mask, I watched the ferry emerge from the azure depths. The blocky hulk slumped on the seafloor, every inch covered in a blanket of fuzzy flora. My scuba instructor swam alongside, then waved for me to follow. Despite recent storms, the Caribbean waters were shockingly clear; divers drifted all around us, circling the corroded vessel and filling the scene with exhaled bubbles.

'The Wreck' lies at a depth of only 40ft (12m) or so, perfect for a novice diver like me. The derelict ferry was deliberately sunk in a well trafficked bay, so it's easy to access by motorboat and free of tragic stories. Yet for me, it might as well have been a Spanish galleon; this was my first encounter with an underwater ruin, and I sighed admiringly into the mouthpiece of my regulator.

Of *course* this all happened in Bocas del Toro, a cluster of islands in the northeast corner of Panama. Literally translated as 'The Bull's Mouth', Bocas is a popular destination for backpackers, who tumble into laid-back hostels and sun themselves on remote beaches. There's a lot to be said for the archipelago's many hammocks and cold bottles of Balboa beer, and I have spent plenty of hours here relaxing in the shade of palm trees. Bocas Town, as many call it, is a colorful village with a smattering of harborside restaurants. Some dining areas are built on old docks, and you can actually hear the waves rippling beneath the floorboards.

But for this traveler, Bocas is also a place of many 'firsts'. On one trip, I hopped on a late-night boat and rode into the mangroves with a diverse group of backpackers. I had never seen the tropical wetlands after dark; when we dipped our hands into the black depths,

Previous pages: Plump red cushion sea stars are jewel-like regular visitors to the shallows around Bocas del Toro. *Above left:* The islands' overwater bungalows offer the ultimate seaside spot. *Above:* Bocas Town, surrounded by reef-rich waters. *Right:* Close encounters with sea stars at Playa Estrella (Star Beach).

DON'T LEAVE WITHOUT ...

1. Savoring a semi-formal dinner at any restaurant along Calle Primera in Bocas Town. Diverse menus and outstanding preparation make it worth trying a different place each night.

2. Motoring out to Playa Estrella, a family-friendly paradise of white sand, glassy waters and chubby cushion starfish relaxing in the shallows.

3. Boating into the mangroves. These labyrinthine ecosystems are mesmerizing during the day, and many tours double as snorkeling expeditions. Bioluminescence is also visible during a new moon.

bioluminescent phytoplankton sparkled around our hands; and then our guide urged us to jump into the balmy water and swim through these living galaxies – magical. Until Bocas del Toro, I'd also never spotted a starfish in real life, let alone one so corpulent, sprawled in the cream-colored shallows of Playa Estrella (Star Beach). I'd never seen a sign marked 'Monkey Crossing', yet there it was, on a road on Isla Bastimentos; and I'd never heard the English-based Creole spoken by the archipelago's Afro-Panamanian residents. It was here that I sliced into my first seared yellowfin tuna steak, and it became a favorite seafood dish. And yes, I earned my Open Water certificate here, practicing my hand signals and flipper strokes in the safety of Bocas' bay.

Bocas del Toro feels remote, like a geographic secret. Nearly 200 miles (322km) west of Panama City, the islands are reachable only by boat or air. At the end of my last visit, I departed by way of a small plane out of José Ezequiel Hall International Airport, with its rustic runway cut into the rainforest. As the propellers whirred and the Cessna lifted over glistening waters, it all slipped beneath clouds, like a dream – a dream I already couldn't wait to have again.

Far left: Overwater accommodation on the shores of Isla Colón, the main island of Bocas del Toro. *Left:* Laid-back life in Bocas Town.

NEW MEETS OLD

IN THIS CULTURE-RICH CAPITAL

Rabat, Morocco

ZARA SEKHAVATI Much less visited than well-loved Marrakesh and Essaouira, Rabat offers travelers something fresh. From historical sites and modern additions on the skyline to garden walks, lively music and soft-sand surf beaches, the country's dynamic capital is one of its most underrated destinations.

The pounding *darbuka* drums make my eardrums pulsate, and as my feet move to the rhythm of the vibrating beats, a cry of 'Welcome to the Mawazine Festival!' rings through the air. It's not the first time I've been overcome by music in Morocco. A Gnaoua concert in Fez was one of those everlasting memories that made me realize the power of travel. That was 15 years ago – and here I am being transformed by the country's extraordinary music once again. Staged over nine days in June, the 90% free Mawazine is the country's biggest music festival, drawing local and international crowds to see Moroccan performers alongside headline global acts.

Energized by shows on the Mawazine stage, I head out to explore the next day. An enticing blend of old and new, Morocco's capital is UNESCO World Heritage–listed for its mix of historic buildings and modern design. In Chellah – an archaeological site which the Phoenicians controlled until around 40 CE, when the Romans took over – I spot a mosque, mosaics, Roman ruins and Latin inscriptions. In the nearby Mausoleum of Mohammed V – resting place of the former Moroccan king and his sons King Hassan II and Prince Abdallah – I admire multicolored *zellige* tilework in intricate geometric patterns and, looking up, the hand-carved cedarwood ceiling, delicately decorated with gold leaf.

I look up to Rabat's skyline, too. At 144ft (44m), I can't miss the Tour Hassan, imagined as part of one of the world's tallest mosques until an earthquake destroyed it in 1755; my hand traces over the surviving jagged-stone pillars. It feels like Rabat never stops building. Recently opened and housing a hotel, apartments and a viewing terrace, the 820ft (250m) Tour Mohammed VI skyscraper is the fourth-tallest building in Africa. I also admire the funky exterior of Théâtre Royal de Rabat (inaugurated in 2024, but still not operational), a fluid

Previous pages, left to right: Rue des Consuls in Rabat's buzzing medina; A perfect view of the River Bou Regreg in Rabat. *Left:* Ultramodern Théâtre Royal de Rabat. *Above:* Rabat's must-see Tour Hassan dates to the late 12th century.

DON'T LEAVE WITHOUT ...

1. Attending a festival; as well as the Mawazine in June, May's Jazz au Chellah and August's Rab'Africa Festival are other highlights of Rabat's musical calendar.

2. Looking out from the Kasbah des Oudaias: the stellar panorama across the Atlantic Ocean and the River Bou Regreg bring peace and tranquility to anyone's itinerary.

3. Exploring Chella's Phoenician and Roman remains and the ornate Mausoleum of Mohammed V to gain insights into Rabat's long and storied history.

Right: Intricate *zellige* tilework adorns buildings across Rabat, such as this water fountain below Tour Hassan. *Above left:* Ceramic pots in production at Complexe de l'Artisanat d'Oulja in nearby Salé. *Above right:* Cooking up to-go meals in the medina.

design by the late Pritzker Prize-winning architect Zaha Hadid. The Villa des Arts, a strikingly white art deco gallery dating from 1929, displays artwork by Moroccan artists. Other landmarks such as the art deco Cinéma Renaissance add to the city's diverse landscape.

One of the simple pleasures in Rabat is walking. In the lavender-scented Andalusian Gardens, I spot orange trees while basking in the morning light. I meander through Kasbah des Oudaias, a 12th-century clifftop citadel that offers blissful views across the Atlantic and the River Bou Regreg. My toes sink into the sand at Plage de Rabat, the main beach and a popular surf spot.

And then there are the souqs. In the medina, Souq es Sebbat is known for its jewelry and Rue des Consuls for traditional *rbati* rugs, made using high-warp looms. In the distance, handcrafted iron castanets transport me to Marrakesh's Djemaa El Fna; a *sintir* (lute) takes me to Essaouira's medina. As I continue through the cobbled alleyways, I hear a *darbuka* drum and its loud beats carry me back instantly to the Mawazine Festival. For that is where Rabat began for me.

59

Gujarat, India

PRACHI JOSHI From sunbaked salt flats to temple-studded towns and the country's longest coastline kissed by the Arabian Sea, Gujarat dazzles with contrasts. It's where lions still roam wild, artisans keep traditional crafts alive and history breathes through every stone. Few places blend heritage, wilderness and warmth quite like India's fifth-largest state.

Start in Ahmedabad (Amdavad), Gujarat's energetic capital of culture, where I like to stroll the immaculately maintained Sabarmati Riverfront and soak up the serenity before diving into the UNESCO-listed old city. Its labyrinthine lanes, centuries-old mosques and *havelis* (mansions, with carved wooden facades) reveal a living heritage that's as compelling as any museum. Speaking of museums, my favorite is Calico Museum of Textiles, which showcases a comprehensive collection of Indian fabrics and regional embroidery. Sign up online for a free morning or evening tour; spaces are limited so do it well in advance.

After a couple of days in Ahmedabad, wider Gujarat is calling – and I like to take in the Modhera–Patan–Sidhpur circuit on a day trip. First stop should be the Sun Temple at Modhera – an architectural masterpiece. I recommend visiting in the morning, when sunlight filters through intricately carved pillars and reflects off the temple's stepped tank; it's a sight that feels almost surreal. Next, drive to Patan, famed for exquisite Patola silk saris and the 11th-century Rani-ki-Vav, a spectacular seven-level step-well adorned with more than a thousand intricately carved sculptures. A short hop away lies Sidhpur, a dusty town that quite improbably holds some of the most ornate *havelis* I have ever seen. These 19th-century European-style houses sport pastel facades, trellised balconies and elaborate stucco work. Few travelers make it here, and that's part of the magic.

Previous pages: Traditional *haveli* mansions line the streets of Sidhpur. *Left:* Modhera's atmospheric Sun Temple. *Right:* Street-food for sale in Ahmedabad's Manek Chowk. *Below:* Champaner-Pavagadh's buildings date from the 11th to the 14th century.

South of Ahmedabad, Vadodara (Baroda) offers a different flavor altogether: the refined elegance of a former princely state. I was gobsmacked when I first saw Lakshmi Vilas Palace. Still home to the Gaekwad family (former royal rulers of Baroda), it's an Indo-Saracenic icon four times the size of Britain's Buckingham Palace. But the real gem nearby is Champaner-Pavagadh Archaeological Park, a UNESCO World Heritage Site where you can walk amid ancient mosques, fort walls and step-wells with hardly another visitor in sight.

My travels in Gujarat wouldn't be complete without a taste of the wild. Gir National Park is the only place in the world where you can see Asiatic lions in their natural habitat. Safaris here are thrilling yet surprisingly accessible, with well-organized tours and comfortable lodges nearby; and given the growing lion population, sightings are fairly common. Finally, I recommend journeying north to the Rann of Kachchh (Kutch), where vast white salt flats stretch to the horizon. If possible, time your visit to coincide with the Rann Utsav (usually late October to early March), a festival celebrating local crafts, music and dance under the moonlit sky. The best way to experience it is to stay in a tent village, where you can enjoy cultural activities, camel rides and local food.

What makes Gujarat remarkable isn't any single sight, but how effortlessly history, craft and wild beauty come together in one unforgettable sweep.

Left main: Dawn over Ahmedabad's waterfront from Sabarmati Ashram, former HQ of Mahatma Gandhi. *Left inset:* The city from above, cut through by the Ahmedabad Metro. *Above:* Filled with spiced lentils, potatos or green peas, *navtad* samosas are an Ahmedabad speciality.

DON'T LEAVE WITHOUT ...

1. Visiting the ancient Indus Valley Civilization sites of Lothal and Dholavira, which offer a rare glimpse into the innovations of one of the world's earliest urban cultures.

2. Admiring the rich and varied craft traditions of Kutch at the world-class museum run by Shrujan Living and Learning Design Centre near Bhuj.

3. Gorging at Manek Chowk, Ahmedabad's lively street-food night market; try experimental fusion dishes – pineapple sandwich or chocolate-cheese dosa, anyone?

PLUNGE INTO THE LAID-BACK
SWEDISH RIVIERA

Skanör-Falsterbo, Sweden

PIA PETERSON HAGGARTY With its quiet streets and rows of wide, white-walled traditional cottages fronted by overspilling gardens, Skanör-Falsterbo is a haven for anyone who wants to slow down and experience a Scandinavian summer. This beach-blessed 'Swedish Riviera' is a perfect seaside escape.

Sitting on a small spit of land reaching out into the south Baltic Sea, just a 35-minute drive south of Malmö and an hour from Copenhagen, Skanör and Falsterbo are two small towns linked by a bridge across a narrow stream. The peninsula first achieved notoriety during the herring age of the 13th century; much later its beaches and mild weather attracted both year-round residents and summer tourists from Malmö. My family visited in August, just at the end of the season. After a plane from New York, the bustle of Stockholm and a high-speed rail journey with a toddler, the peaceful streets in Skanör were a revelation – I have never breathed calmer, cleaner air.

There are a handful of lovely old-style hotels in the area, and we treated ourselves to a stay at the contemporary-styled Gässlingen, where we could spend our days in and out of the pool, hot tub and sauna. The hotel's location at the north end of the peninsula also made it easy to take walks down to the sea, and into the nature preserve that encompasses most of the coast. We followed a grassy path along the shoreline for 5.5 miles (9km) to the tip of the peninsula, passing rows and rows of small wooden bathing shacks. Along the way, we also glimpsed the area's three golf courses – and even if you're not a golfer, dropping in for a pint at the Falsterbo Golfklubb pub is the perfect way to cap an afternoon walk.

It wouldn't be the Swedish Riviera without a sea to dip in. The wooden bathing shacks may be privately owned, and the Baltic Sea is chilly – but that shouldn't stop you from bringing a towel and enjoying a dip off the Falsterbo Brygga, a swimming pier built far out into the water on the peninsula's southeast side. Before or after the beach, stop by nearby Kust Falsterbo for lunch or for *fika* – the traditional Swedish coffee-and-cake break (try the apple cake, if it's available). And though the herring have long been fished out of the

Previous pages: Signs directing visitors to fresh fish at the the Skanör marina. *Left:* Clogs from Falsterbotofflan sit at the end of the Falsterbo brygga swimming pier. *Below:* People enjoying the late summer sun along the edge of the Baltic in Falsterbo.

DON'T LEAVE WITHOUT ...

1. Delving in to both the old and the new: Danish and Swedish history at the Falsterbo Museum, and contemporary art at the Falsterbo Photo Art Museum.

2. Visiting a sauna: grab a day pass for the swish oceanside Kallbadhus, where you can sweat it out and then take a cold plunge in the sea.

3. Enjoying the Swedish specialty *kardemummabullar* (cardamom buns); pick them up from the coffee cart which sets up along the peninsula's main road in the summer.

Left: A garden in downtown Skanör. *Below:* A family walking out to Falsterbo brygga. *Right:* Rear view of the bathing huts that line the shore along the peninsula.

Baltic, the region's seafaring culture is still alive at Fiskhuset Skanör, a seafood restaurant over on the peninsula's northwest. We enjoyed fish and chips, and of course cured-salmon *gravlax* with dill potatoes, and also picked up some seafood treats to go.

One of the most charming things about Skanör-Falsterbo is the local obsession with geese – you can't escape tributes to these waddling residents. The beloved local geese are celebrated annually with the Gåsaloppet, a Midsummer's Eve event consisting of races and a fair in the town center. The residents' enthusiasm for their feathered neighbors is memorialized on the clogs sold at Falsterbotofflan, which staff adorn with a hand-painted goose; you can also opt to have them personalized with your name.

While the Baltic is chillier than that other Riviera – the Côte d'Azur – and the towns are much quieter than St-Tropez, a summer stop along the Swedish Riviera absolutely delivered on some of the most relaxing and peaceful moments of my year.

M
MAISON
MARGAN
370 B

Québec, Canada

JOEL BALSAM Canada's largest province has Europe's charm with North America's edge and natural wonders. Immerse yourself in French-Canadian history and culture while wandering the cobblestone streets of Montréal and Québec City – or venture beyond to see whales, climb mountains and sip natural wine. You don't know Canada unless you've visited Québec.

Québec is a must-visit any year, but 2027 is particularly enticing for a string of new and expanded experiences, as well as landmark anniversaries.

In Montréal, celebrate the 60th anniversary of Expo 67, a world fair that transformed the city into a multicultural powerhouse of innovation. Walk, cycle and cross-country ski around Parc Jean-Drapeau, set on a string of islands transformed for Expo 67 and easily accessible via Montréal's excellent metro system. My dad went to the expo every single day and loved to show me photo slides of the fairgrounds – including the still-standing US Pavilion, a geodesic dome that now houses the Biosphère environmental exhibits. These days, I love to gaze at the Expo 67 site from the banks of the St Lawrence River while watching the fireworks displays of L'International des Feux – on every Thursday and Sunday at 10pm from June 26 to July 31. The festival is celebrating its 40th anniversary in 2027, so gear up for a particularly explosive spectacle.

Québec City – turning 420 in 2027 – is a dream for lovers of history, with its winding cobblestone streets, stone fortresses and Canada's oldest standing structures, dating to the early 17th century. It's also the perfect place for just plain lovers: a romantic trip to Québec City within months of dating was a contributing factor in my parents' decision to get married. Catch one of the new immersive light shows inside the city's Église St-Roch or at the impressive shrine of Basilique Ste-Anne-de-Beaupré.

For a taste of Québec without the crowds, venture beyond the major cities. See the province's vast and rugged landscapes via boat – Montréal's first winter cruises are launching in early 2027. Or take the century-old Train de

Previous pages: Boutique shopping in Old Montréal. *Above left:* Gaspésie, Quebec. *Above:* Now housing environmental exhibits, Montréal's Biosphère sits on the former Expo 67 site. *Right:* Devour artisan bagels and much, much more in foodie-friendly Montréal.

DON'T LEAVE WITHOUT ...

1. Embracing Montréal's *joie de vivre* at its many summer festivals – from urban art at Mural and comedy fest Just for Laughs to the Festival International de Jazz de Montréal.

2. Dining on gourmet and traditional cuisine under warm, tinkly lights in Québec City – where the streets are especially atmospheric during the Winter Carnival (held in January or February).

3. Driving or cycling past New England–style cottages to the Cantons de l'Est (Eastern Townships) – Québec's wine region – to taste natural wine, ice cider and local cheeses.

Charlevoix railway along the northern banks of the St Lawrence River to visit the new Espace Hubert-Reeves, a science center located inside a crater where a meteorite crashed 450 million years ago.

Further north, Parc Marin du Saguenay–St-Laurent – already Québec's largest protected marine area – will be expanded to some 1737 sq miles (4500 sq km). That's great news for the hundreds of beluga, humpback, minke and fin whales that feed in the mouth of the Saguenay Fjord every year. Spot them from Parks Canada viewpoints on the Côte-Nord (North Shore), or on a whale-watching cruise from Tadoussac – prime viewing is from June to September.

You can also spy whales along the Côte-Sud (South Shore) of the St Lawrence. Stop along the scenic drive to photograph 19th-century lighthouses, learn about devastating shipwrecks, stay in colorful fishing villages and eat bowls of lobster-loaded poutine (fries, smothered in brown gravy and squeaky cheese curds). And don't miss detour-worthy Parc National de la Gaspésie, which turns 90 in 2027 and is one of few places in southern Canada where you can spot moose and caribou in the wild.

Far left: Husky sledding near Rawdon, northern Québec. *Left:* Music fans throng the streets during the summertime Festival International de Jazz de Montréal.

SLOW TRAVEL
WITH CARIBBEAN SOUL

Montserrat

NERISSA GOLDEN Montserrat is the quiet Caribbean island most travelers overlook, but I promise, once you arrive, you'll wonder how it stayed off your radar for so long. With emerald peaks, black-sand beaches, award-winning dining and a history shaped by fire, this is a destination that leaves you feeling like you've uncovered something rare.

The first sight of Montserrat always awakens my sense of wonder. Lush mountains, wrapped in rainforest and mist, beckon me even before the plane's wheels touch down. This is my sanctuary.

Mornings here are for hiking forest trails before the heat sets in, and evenings for claiming a stretch of beach so quiet I can hear the waves sigh. In between, my island naturally slows me down: rain tapping gently on roofs, roosters insisting it's morning whenever they please, neighbors waving from passing cars. It's unfiltered Caribbean life, restorative and beautifully simple. Whenever friends tell me they're thinking about visiting, I give them the same advice: book at least two or three nights. Montserrat isn't a place you rush through. It's a place that rewards you for slowing down.

One of the first things I do when I'm home is book a spa session. The day-spas here aren't glossy, resort-style retreats; they're tucked into hilltops, gardens and breezy verandas, where Montserrat's natural beauty becomes part of the therapy. My favorite is Blyss Day Spa in Drummonds. Owner Lauretta uses plants from her garden, scented oils and carefully curated treatments to fix what ails you. She always sends me back into the world feeling lighter. And once I'm in the north, a stop at Carr's Bay Corner is non-negotiable. There's nothing like drinking coconut water straight from the nut, then scooping out the delicious jelly inside. Wander the area and you'll find someone bubbling a pot of *ital* (vegetarian) food or frying fish, and a group deep into a dominoes game. Pull up a chair. Moments like these aren't planned – they find you.

And the food? You'll eat exceptionally well, as cooking is an act of love here. Sure, there are the roadside grills and rum shops (and you should stop at every one), but we also have some real culinary standouts – like Olveston House.

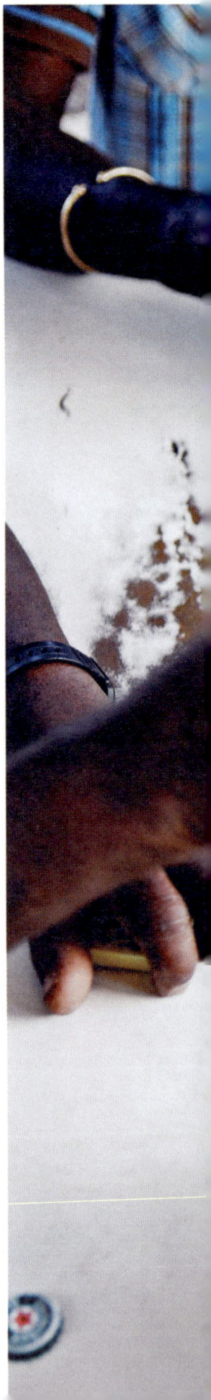

Previous pages: Lovely Little Bay, on Montserrat's northwest coast. *Left:* Stop off at nearby Carr's Bay Corner to sip coconut water straight from the nut, fuel up on delicious local specialties and sit down with the regulars for a spirited game of dominos.

DON'T LEAVE WITHOUT ...

1. Drinking refreshing natural spring water from Runaway Ghaut; pause for a sip here and legend says you'll return to Montserrat.

2. Stopping by the People's Place at Hilltop for sweeping northern views and one essential taste of Montserrat: Uncle John's goat water, a rich savory stew that's the island's national dish.

3. Seeing the Buried City from St George's Hill – from where the volcano feels almost touchable, and the view of Plymouth is reverent, haunting and unforgettable.

Right: The former capital of Plymouth, had been buried buried under a thick deposit of volcanic ash. *Above left:* Montserrat's smoking Soufrière Hills Volcano. *Above right:* Away from the volcano, Montserrat delivers on laid-back Caribbean living.

It sits in the former home of Sir George Martin, the legendary Beatles manager and founder of Air Studios, where so many iconic '80s hits were recorded. Dining there feels like stepping into music history wrapped in Caribbean warmth. Then there's Isles Bay Beach Bar, ranked among the Caribbean's top ten beach bars – the perfect spot for sunset cocktails, grilled seafood and the occasional live music night that becomes a delightful memory.

Of course, Montserrat's story includes its volcanic past. The eruptions from 1995 to 2010 reshaped the island, leaving the former capital Plymouth frozen in time under layers of ash. Every time I take visitors on a tour, whether by land or by boat, I'm reminded of nature's power and the tenacious spirit of our people.

But Montserrat isn't defined by loss. It's defined by life. The rainforest is teeming with unlikely, almost mystical critters, some still being discovered and studied. The reefs are vibrant. The people are warm, witty and fiercely proud. And because visitor numbers are small, you will never feel like a tourist here; you'll feel like my guest, welcomed into a story that is still being written.

TOURING THE WORLD'S TALLEST TREES

California's Coastal Redwoods, USA

BECCA HUNT The drama of the Northern Californian coast isn't just beaches and cliffsides. Coastal redwoods – the tallest trees on Earth – are also found here, and they are staggering to see. Along with Jurassic-sized ferns, tinsel-like moss, vibrant rhododendrons, mysterious mushrooms and bright yellow banana slugs, wandering among the towering trees feels like going back in time.

Redwood trees dot the San Francisco Bay Area where my partner and I live with our six-year-old, but the magnificent specimens up north in Humboldt Redwoods and Jedediah Smith Redwoods State Parks dwarf our local biggies.

On a recent offseason trip in February, we debated on seeing the Avenue of the Giants, a dreamlike highway and gateway to the parks – but it was well worth it, even if it took us a little off track. Then it was into Humboldt for old-growth redwoods, especially massive trees that are centuries-old, up to 300ft (90m) tall and often contain their own ecosystems, habitats and even animal life. Take deep breaths in these oxygen-rich woods, and even during summer, prepare for the constant drip and drizzle from the treetops. Pack a bag of snacks and plenty of water – you'll want to explore the trails for longer than you think.

You can only crane your neck so much, so we spent time up close with the more accessible fallen trees. Their exposed roots look like exploding fireworks, and you'll often see a host of mushroom varieties and other plant life growing on the trunks. Amble along the paths to see some famous giants, and soak in the lush forest. Even with a kid in tow, we only needed a day and a half in Humboldt to see a lot.

For a break from the redwoods, we visited Fern Canyon. A short hike in from a parking lot, it's a small, storybook-like ravine carpeted with ferns on both sides, water dripping down like a living wall in a fancy hotel. Season depending,

Previous pages, left to right: Sunlight pouring in through the towering redwood trees along the Boy Scout trail, Jedidiah Smith Redwoods State Park. *Left:* The verdant lushness of Fern Canyon. *Right:* Fungi can flourish in the damp redwood forest. *Below:* New life grows atop old along the Mill Creek Trail.

hike through a few inches or more of water for a fun and enchanting family-friendly adventure. Even with high water and pouring rain, I'd do it again (but with better rain boots).

Next, we headed up to Crescent City, an unassuming place with lovely beaches, whales spouting everywhere and a neat lighthouse – all just minutes from the parks.

After a glimpse of the uniquely clear Smith River nearby, we drove on along the network of narrow, winding roads in Jedediah Smith Redwoods State Park to get to the Boy Scout Trail. The park has tons of entry points and landmarks: Stout Grove, Mill Creek, Grove of Titans, Hiouchi and more. If you can, hike the entire 5.5-mile (9km) loop at Boy Scout. Our most magical day was following the trail out and back as far as our kid could manage – no famous trees in mind. The rain had stopped and sunlight was beaming through the tall trees. This was capped off with a stop at the Battery Point Lighthouse for a change of scenery, some local history and a stunning sunset.

With the limitation of little legs, we mostly made it to the 1-mile (1.6km) loops to seek out the most famous trees – but with so much to see at every turn, it's hard to go wrong in this neck of the woods.

Left: Wild, wave-whipped coastline near Crescent City, from where whales can sometimes be spotted from the shore. *Above:* Titanic trees abound in Humboldt Redwoods and Jedediah Smith Redwoods State Parks.

DON'T LEAVE WITHOUT ...

1. Heading to Fern Canyon or other nearby spots for different flora and fauna and even different weather; there's no need to limit yourself to the redwoods.

2. Setting aside time to be still, breathe deeply and take it all in – the redwoods are refreshingly peaceful.

3. Visiting a forest-fringed beach. Even (or especially) on a cold, gray day, it's fun to experience the woods and the water; and keep an eye out for whales year-round.

Oman

DR JENNY WALKER With spectacular desert landscapes and a mountain range that, topping 10,000ft (3040m), is as high as the coastline is long, Oman is a joy for adventurous travelers. But the most memorable part of a trip here is meeting the hospitable Omani people, who make a virtue of cherishing their visitors.

Spreading a mat over the arid mountain top, an elderly man arranges a Thermos (Omani coffeepot of choice), three tiny cups and a parcel of sticky, sesame-seeded dates. He takes off his shoes, kneels on the mat and commences the important business of rinsing cups. 'Come! Drink *qahwa*,' he says to us in Arabic, as if it's perfectly normal to see a pair of foreigners crest the perilous top of his remote mountain aerie, on a track barely big enough for goats. We cover the customary pleasantries – a routine of five minutes, returned to frequently throughout conversations here. 'How's the family? What's the news? No news? That's good.' At length, our limited Arabic exhausted, our host begins his life story ('When I was a pilot in the Air Force...'), in perfect English.

This was a decade ago, admittedly, when my husband and I were writing a book about similar off-road goat tracks in Oman. Much has changed since then, including the paving of many of the routes, but what hasn't changed is the guaranteed welcome. Hospitality is written into the social fabric of Omani society, and whether you're being greeted by a man of the mountains or attending an official meeting, coffee, dates and small talk are indispensable to the concept of *marhaban* (meaning 'welcome').

With a history of maritime empire tempered by the Bedouin necessity of getting along with strangers, Omanis have had plenty of practice in refining interactions with others. A sizable part of the population traces its origins to Balochistan, in today's Pakistan; others speak Swahili from a youth spent in East Africa; many older Omanis were educated abroad. Combine this globalized demographic with the expats who form the backbone of local commerce, and it's easy to see how the country has become a respected, outward-looking regional peacekeeper – albeit understated in nature.

Understatement is an appropriate term for many other aspects of the Oman experience. Go looking for the tallest

Previous pages, left to right: Desert camp at a Sharqiya Sands; Intricate tilework at Muscat's Grand Mosque. *Left:* State-of-the-art Oman Across Ages Museum near Nizwa. *Below:* Misfat, a traditional village in the mountainous north of Oman.

DON'T LEAVE WITHOUT ...

1. Hiking up at least one *wadi* (river valley), where running water attracts kingfishers and butterflies, and where ancient *aflaj* (irrigation channels) water terraced gardens of date palms.

2. Journeying over the smooth contours of sand on camel-back in the Sharqiya Sands – corridors of silvery dunes, just a two-hour drive from Muscat.

3. Tracing Oman's seafaring heritage in the capital's museums and the boatyards of Sur, then take to the water to swim with turtles and shoals of sardines.

Below left: A Bedouin leads his camels across the Sharqiya Sands. *Below*: Take time out from Oman's cities to wander lush *wadis* watered by ancient *aflaj* channels. *Right*: Discover Omani maritime heritage in seaside Sur.

and most audacious and you'll be better served visiting Oman's wealthy neighbors. Seek quality over ostentation, though – as showcased in the Grand Mosque, National Museum and Royal Opera House in capital Muscat – and you'll be touching on a source of national pride.

Carefully nurtured by the late, much-beloved Sultan Qaboos bin Said, nationhood has been key to the country's rapid advancement since 1970. Step into the Renaissance Gallery in high-tech Oman Across Ages Museum, near Nizwa, and you'll notice Omani women and men standing that bit taller as they recognize their own part in growing today's robust infrastructure, education and health-care. This renaissance has been achieved not through change alone, but through knowing what parts of the past to keep. Today, visitors to the northern mountains, coastal dunes and southern leopard lands will find landscapes laced with human stories, told in petroglyphs and ancient burial sites, through restored forts, terraced villages and aged date plantations. It's this continuity of culture, built on a respect for heritage, religion and family, that makes Oman the self-assured success it is today.

UNCROWDED SAFARI MAGIC IN THE RED PLAINS

Tsavo East and West National Parks, Kenya

HARRIET AKINYI Thanks to their vast red-earth savannas, enormous elephant herds, dramatic lava flows and quiet, crowd-free horizons, the neighboring national parks of Tsavo East and West offer a raw, soul stirring adventure. Here, wildlife feels wilder, landscapes seem endless and every sunrise or sunset carries the thrill of true African wilderness.

The first thing you feel when you visit Tsavo is space. Kenya's wild and fiery heart has an almost overwhelming, breath-stealing vastness that settles into your chest the moment you arrive. Tsavo East feels wide open – like the land has pulled back its curtains on endless plains where baobabs stand like watchful elders and red-dusted elephants move across the horizon. On the other side of the highway, volcanic Tsavo West feels entirely different – darker and moodier. The Earth shows its scars in black lava fields and hidden springs, while distant Mt Kilimanjaro's snow-capped silhouette stands sentinel and the gentle, emerald waves of the Chyulu Hills soften the harsh plains. And with Tsavo West's new rhino sanctuary (opened in 2025) representing a major step in protecting the park's black rhinos, these twin reserves are a must-visit for travelers seeking raw adventure, big landscape and revived conservation.

Exploring both parks in one trip is like experiencing two personalities of the same wilderness, each powerful in its own way. But wherever you roam (in the company of trained guides), you'll bed down by night in comfortable luxury: canvas tents with big beds, open-air showers warmed by the sun and dining decks overlooking watering holes where wildlife gathers.

Tsavo is the kind of Africa that lives in the imagination long before flights are booked and passports stamped – but nothing prepares you for how fully it surrounds you once you get there. On my first evening, the air was scented with dust and wild sage. The sky stretched wider than any I've seen, and the silence – broken only by distant elephant rumbles or the echoes of guinea fowl – felt almost sacred.

Previous pages: Follow red-earth roads to wonderful wildlife in Tsavo West. *Above left:* Hippos wallow in Tsavo West's crystal-clear Mzima Springs. *Above and right:* Large herds of elephant roam the savannas of Tsavo East.

DON'T LEAVE WITHOUT ...

1. Visiting Tsavo West's recently opened rhino sanctuary, to witness conservation in action and directly contribute to maintaining populations of critically endangered black rhino.

2. Watching the sun dip over the savanna from Poacher's Lookout in Tsavo West, as elephants and giraffes roam below and cocktails are served – a perfect evening ritual.

3. Browsing wares made by local Kamba woodcarvers at the Tsavo West gate; purchases directly support the local community.

In Tsavo East, I witnessed scale. Herds of elephants, sometimes numbering up to 100, moved in slow unison. The open terrain gave a clear view of buffalo and giraffe; the lucky might even glimpse an elusive cheetah sprinting across the plains. Sunrise was unforgettable: a molten red sun rising over Yatta Plateau (the longest lava flow on Earth), with the Chyulu Hills adding layers of green and gold to the skyline. At Lugard Falls, a roaring rush of water carved wild shapes into ancient rocks, while Aruba Dam was an afternoon magnet for the park's elephants.

Tsavo West surprised me with contrasts. It's home to Mzima Springs, a crystalline oasis fed by an underground reservoir beneath the Chyulu Hills. Standing at its edge, watching hippos drift like submerged boulders and various species of fish swirl in turquoise water, felt like stumbling into a secret world. And at the Shetani Lava Flow, I gazed out over a massive field of volcanic black rocks born from a centuries-old eruption.

It took me five days to fully explore both parks. By the time I left, my safari boots were dusted red, and my heart and my camera's memory card were full thanks to the memories made during my tour. Tsavo is wild, transformative and profoundly alive. It's the kind of place that stays with you long after you've boarded your flight home.

Far left: Tsavo East's Lugard Falls, where the rushing Galana River has gouged out fantastical shapes. *Left:* Zebra gather on the grasslands of Tsavo East.

THE WILD WEST OF THE SOUTH PACIFIC

New Caledonia

JESSICA LOCKHART As well as being a region rich in Melanesian and Polynesian traditions, the South Pacific has long been synonymous with the sweet life in the minds of travellers: Tiki-style cocktails, colorful coral gardens and even more vibrant cultural shows. New Caledonia breaks the mold entirely, blending French and Indigenous culture with scenes straight out of the Wild West.

I'm standing in the bed of a truck, clinging tightly to the roll bars as it climbs higher through the pasture. From the farm's highest point, mountains spread out in the distance – and then I see them: a massive herd of wild deer, bounding through the fields. Soon, we reach the property's boundary on the shores of the Coral Sea. In a seawater canal, a dark shadow flits beneath the surface, poking its head up briefly for air. Never did I expect to see a green sea turtle swimming on a massive cattle station – but it's far from the first surprise that New Caledonia has offered up.

As Lonely Planet's Destination Editor for Oceania, I've traveled and worked widely across the South Pacific, which is why it was easy to make assumptions when I booked my flights and looked at the map. New Caledonia's geography alone felt familiar: Grande Terre, the baguette-shaped main island, is surrounded by smaller islands, coral reefs and lagoons, not unlike neighboring Vanuatu. But this French overseas territory – just a two-hour flight from Brisbane, Australia – soon subverted everything I thought I knew about the region, in the best possible way.

Sure, you can sleep in overwater bungalows (head to Îlot Maître, a 25-minute ferry ride from the capital, Nouméa) and spend days lazing on white-sand beaches or snorkeling beside turtles in twinkling turquoise seas (the islands of Lifou and L'Île-des-Pins are two of the most popular spots to do so). Or for something more active, kitesurfing is the sport of choice, with world champions like Tom Hebert proudly calling New Caledonia home.

But this is also a place where Broussard (French cowboy) culture runs deep. Brahman cattle graze on red-earth savannas amongst eucalypts, sharing their pastures with shrimp farms that push up against mangroves. Every August, up to 30,000 people flock to Grande Terre's west coast for Foire

Previous pages: Overwater bungalows in Îlot Maître. *Left:* Sailing a traditional outrigger canoe offshore of L'Île-des-Pins is an unforgettable experience. *Above:* Tropical flair in the gardens of Gîte Wankos, Grande Terre.

DON'T LEAVE WITHOUT ...

1. Sailing on a traditional outrigger canoe through the rock islands of Upi Bay in L'Île-des-Pins (Island of Pines).

2. Sitting down to a meal at La Table du Banian outside La Foa, where every ingredient is local – from the fish to the fruit grown in the property's garden.

3. Hiking through Parc des Grandes Fougères (Great Ferns Park), a massive expanse of rainforest that's home to endemic flora and fauna, including the cagou – a bluish-gray flightless bird.

Right: Preparing *bougna*, a traditional Kanak dish. *Above left:* Shoreside perfection on Îlot Maître. *Above right:* Surrounded by sculpted poles, L'Île-des-Pins' Saint-Maurice Monument symbolizes harmony between traditional beliefs and Christianity.

de Bourail, a celebration of the region's rich agricultural heritage with meat-cutting, sheep shearing and whip-cracking competitions. The rest of the year, visitors can get a taste of *la brousse* (bush or rural) spirit at one of the region's homestays, such as Gîte Les Nautilus, where you'll likely be treated to venison stew. Don't be surprised if you're inspired to saddle up and trot down the beach with operators like Far West Ranch.

One of my most memorable adventures, however, was along the 'baguette's' ear – a spine of rolling green mountains cutting down Grande Terre's center, reaching heights of up to 5300ft (1615m). This is where I spend my day with Rosana Monefara, a member of the Koindé tribe. At her guesthouse Gîte Wankos, we stand side by side grating green bananas and taro to prepare *bougna*, a traditional Kanak dish of veggies and chicken baked in a banana-leaf wrap. As the food simmers away in a coconut broth, Rosana takes me to cool off in a nearby waterfall. I gaze up at the rushing water around me. Yes, this reminds me of the South Pacific – yet it's unlike anything I've experienced before.

EXPERIENCES

DIVE INTO
WILD ANTARCTIC SEAS
ULSTEIN
aurora
expeditions

Take a polar plunge

Antarctica

BREKKE FLETCHER Of all the things I've ever done, hurling myself from a Zodiac inflatable boat into the Southern Ocean off the Antarctic Peninsula is the most extreme. The intensity of anticipatory adrenaline was immediately overwhelmed by the shock of penetrating 32°F (0°C) water. I'll never be the same.

I read Alfred Lansing's *Endurance: Shackleton's Extraordinary Voyage* in one sitting. This is not a boast or a brag, but evidence of the birth of an obsession. Overcome by the harrowing nature of the expedition, I got lost in the evocative descriptions of the powerful forces at play, one being Sir Ernest Shackleton himself. This is a tale of man versus nature, the perils of exploration - and of bravado, hubris, confidence, never giving up and never giving in.

Over a century later, this and other Antarctic expeditions continue to enthrall me. I've longed for a (safe) taste of that spirit of exploration, partaking - even in a small way - in an Antarctic journey, and finding a way to make the experience of being so close to the South Pole my own.

What follows is hardly harrowing. Once I booked my (fancy) Antarctic cruise, my primary objective - outside of landing on the continent, seeing penguins, seals, whales, icebergs and glaciers - was to participate in a polar plunge.

I've done some cold-plunging in the Irish Sea and the Deschutes River in Oregon, but nothing could have prepared me for the severity of jumping into freezing water, surrounded by bobbing icebergs and calving glaciers.

To say the weather during an Antarctic cruise is unpredictable is to wildly understate the case. Days can start out with 50mph (80km/h) winds and zero visibility, and end with near-blinding brightness and blue skies. You'll wake to a sea that looks like glass, only to find yourself

Previous pages: Gentoo penguins on Cuverville Island. *Left:* Humpback whales gather off Antarctica to gorge on krill. *Right:* Icebergs at Cierva Cove, on the west coast of Graham Land. *Below:* The author prepares for her plunge.

hanging on for dear life as the ship lists from the power of two concurrent storms suddenly whipping up intense winds and swells on either side of the vessel.

Because the conditions for plunging must be precisely perfect, it wasn't until day seven of our 10-day voyage that we were allowed to dive in Neko Harbour, a breathtaking inlet discovered by Belgian explorer Adrien de Gerlache in the early 20th century. I won't lie and say I wasn't hoping that conditions would never be perfect, so that I wouldn't have to go through with it.

When my time came to take the plunge – literally – into the bay, my heart was in my throat. A kind, smiling, seen-it-all crew member offered me a shot of brandy, which I gulped in one go. I stripped down to my bathing suit and bare feet and allowed the crew to secure my waist with a harness before stepping onto the starboard side of the Zodiac from which I flung myself.

I yelped when I jumped, holding my breath as I smashed through the surface. My mind swirled as I tried to outthink the pain (described perfectly by Jack in *Titanic*: 'It hits you like a thousand knives stabbing you all over your body.') and savor the ephemeral moment before frantically racing to the ladder to climb back on board. One of the most powerful sensations of my life lasted only 10 seconds, but it's forever imprinted on my heart and in my mind.

Left main: Sailing through icy waters in the Antarctic Sound. *Left inset:* Weddell seal at Charlotte Bay. *Above:* An unforgettable moment as the author takes the (icy) plunge.

DON'T LEAVE WITHOUT ...

1. Chatting with the crew, who possess expertise across every relevant field of study possible. I never thought I could be captivated by a lecture on krill.

2. Seeing gentoos and chinstraps waddle along 'penguin superhighways'. We were also lucky enough to see a single emperor penguin holding court on an iceberg.

3. Scanning for whales: the sound of water shooting up through a humpback's blowhole is the best indicator that you'll be seeing one surface to breathe.

MASTERPIECES OF ART AND ARCHITECTURE

Visit Abu Dhabi's museums

United Arab Emirates

BREKKE FLETCHER I'm not sure what I expected from Abu Dhabi, other than high rises and high-octane action. What utterly astonished me was the breathtaking architecture of this ever-evolving city's cultural institutions. I marveled at gleaming buildings designed by masters such as Jean Nouvel, whose Louvre Abu Dhabi is so stunningly beautiful, it can be hard to believe.

Abu Dhabi's Saadiyat Island (which translates to 'Island of Happiness') is the nexus of the city's 21st-century renaissance, with a concentrated Cultural District that's home to the UAE's most enthralling arts institutions. Manarat Al Saadiyat is a community-focused complex that hosts exhibitions, creative workshops and film screenings. A stone's throw away, David Adjaye's striking Abrahamic Family House is a paean to interfaith tolerance and education, housing a synagogue, a church and a mosque.

But for me, the district's most exquisite showpiece is the Louvre Abu Dhabi, designed by Pritzker Prize-winning architect Jean Nouvel. I can easily convey its proportions: its gargantuan white dome of 7850 intersecting stars of variable size and composition, its 55 rooms, including 23 galleries, surrounded on three sides by undulating Arabian waters. What is more difficult – and perhaps impossible – to describe is what it feels like to be standing under that intricate and exquisite dome, turning circles in the main hall and following narrow interconnected paths dotted with windows offering views across the water to other areas of the museum. The most apt (and admittedly most dramatic) way to explain its effect is Stendhal syndrome: awe, wonder and disbelief coursed through my body like an elliptical electrical current as unbeckoned tears wet my face.

Within the museum are 600 works that span centuries, from the Paleolithic era to the present day. Galleries are curated by epoch, juxtaposing the artistic modalities and themes across the globe over time. As befits the Louvre partnership, works by canonical masters – such as Édouard Manet's *The Bohemian* (1861–2) and Piet Mondrian's *Composition with Blue, Red, Yellow and Black* (1922) – are part of the permanent collection.

In 2025, two new museums opened in the Cultural District, both as culturally and architecturally significant as the

Previous pages: A bird's eye view of the Louvre Abu Dhabi's filigreed roof. *Left:* The museum building appears to float above the Gulf waters that surround it. *Below:* The Louvre Abu Dhabi exhibits artworks from ancient civilizations to the present day.

DON'T LEAVE WITHOUT ...

1. Visiting Qasr Al Hosn, Abu Dhabi's oldest stone structure. Built in the 1790s and now a museum, this living memorial delivers a taste of the city's past.

2. Eating at Erth, a perfect spot to have lunch; enjoy superb modern Emirati cuisine in stylish surroundings, just steps from Qasr Al Hosn.

3. Touring Qasr Al Watan: the working presidential palace exemplifies excess and artistry, from the Great Hall to the library and 'Presidential Gifts' room.

Below left: The sweeping interior of Norman Foster–designed Zayed National Museum. *Below:* Artfully displayed exhibits at Natural History Museum Abu Dhabi, designed by Dutch architecture firm Mecanoo. *Right:* Zayed National Museum's sail-like towers echo a falcon in flight.

Louvre. Zayed National Museum focuses on the history and origins of the United Arab Emirates and is a tribute to the country's founding father, Sheikh Zayed bin Sultan Al Nahyan. Designed by another star architect, Norman Foster, its five sail-like towers evoke a falcon in flight. Inside you'll discover thousands of artifacts, installations and sensory experiences that elucidate the history of the UAE.

The gargantuan Natural History Museum Abu Dhabi, by Dutch architecture firm Mecanoo, is as ambitious as it is massive – a suitable size for exploring millions of years of history. A jaw-dropping 82ft (25m) blue whale specimen and 'Stan' the T-Rex skeleton are among its crowd-pleasing displays.

And there's more to come. The world-renowned art juggernaut Frieze made its Abu Dhabi debut in late 2026. A seemingly limitless passion for and investment in art, artists and cultural institutions casts Abu Dhabi as a cultural powerhouse of opulence, energy and elegance. In fact it's so unbelievable, you'll have to see for yourself.

Savor the slow road

Minnesota, USA

BAILEY FREEMAN The scenic route between Minneapolis and the Boundary Waters Canoe Wilderness Area offers a dreamy meander up the North Shore, Minnesota's access point to the spectacular Lake Superior. Here, you get it all: Indigenous and immigrant history, shoreside outdoor adventures and a window into some of the wildest places in the USA.

I'm practically a career roadtripper – I'm a pro at linking together destinations into adventures, and efficiency is kind of my thing. So when I sat down to plan my 320-mile (515km) trip up Minnesota's North Shore, I was surprised to see that my usual day-here-day-there plans simply wouldn't work. Almost every accommodation had a multi-night minimum – and it was the best thing that could have happened.

From Minneapolis, I headed north and made my first stop in sweet little Duluth. This gateway to Lake Superior is perched high on the hills where Minnesota meets Wisconsin and the St Louis River meets the mighty lake itself. Duluth keeps one foot planted in its multi-faceted past and one looking to a progressive future. History buffs will enjoy the story behind Fitger's Brewery (established in 1857) and the comprehensive Lake Superior Railroad Museum; lovers of the arts shouldn't miss catching an edgy theater show at Zeitgeist. If you'd rather stay outdoors, go raptor-spotting at Hawk Ridge or fishing on the nearby Knife River. Once you've knocked all that off your list, it's time to head up the scenic Hwy 61 to the North Shore itself.

And this is where Minnesota's magnificent north begins to unfurl before you. Lake Superior extends like a shimmering mirror to your right while dense Northwoods forests press in on the left. I stopped over near Two Harbors (in a hotel made of boxcars) to rock-scramble at Gooseberry Falls State Park, take in the views at Tettegouche State Park and relax riverside at Temperance River State Park.

Next, I spent some time in the charming lakeside town of Grand Marais, which evolved from an Indigenous trading settlement to a

Previous pages, left to right: Split Rock Lighthouse at Silver Bay, on Lake Superior's North Shore; Hawk Ridge, Duluth. *Above left:* Shoreside forests of Boundary Waters' Sitka Lake harbor moose and wolves. *Above:* Palisade Head, Tettegouche State Park. *Right:* Paddling through the wilderness in Boundary Waters.

DON'T LEAVE WITHOUT ...

1. Taking a sunrise cruise in Duluth – watching the orange sun come up over Lake Superior is pure magic.

2. Grabbing a piece of pie from the famous Rustic Inn near Gooseberry Falls State Park – order from the truck outside and enjoy your slice on the restaurant's porch or take it to go as a picnic snack.

3. Biting into a pillowy treat from Grand Marais' World's Best Donuts. The name may very well be true.

lumber town to an artist commune – dive into a homestyle breakfast at the Blue Water Cafe before perusing Grand Marais' many galleries.

From there, I made a beeline north on the historic Gunflint Trail into the Boundary Waters; Minnesota's northernmost protected area features over 1000 lakes connected by canoe routes. The quiet here soothed like a balm – the aspens chimed in the breeze while the lakes softly lapped against their shores, and everything slowed way, way down. I booked into the cozy Borderland Lodge and reveled in peaceful mornings from the porch, coffee in hand, watching bald eagles swirl in the sky above. Paddle out onto one of the lakes and maybe, just maybe, you'll spot a moose in the marshes; wolves might also make appearances in the autumn and winter. This is a land to be relished – don't rush.

Once you've had your fill of Minnesota's wilderness (for now, at least), make your return to Minneapolis, the state's buzzy capital. Wander the avant-garde galleries of Northeast Arts District, dive into beautiful Indigenous cuisine at the renowned Owanmi, enjoy sunset at one of the city's many municipal parks. It's a perfect punctuation to one of the country's most unique road trips.

Far left: The Third Avenue Bridge over the Mississippi River threads toward the downtown district of Minneapolis, Minnesota's thriving capital. *Left:* Enjoy craft ales at historic Fitger's Brewery, a Duluth institution since 1857.

A BEAUTIFUL BUT UNSUNG
BRITISH PILGRIMAGE ROUTE

Walk St Cuthbert's Way to Lindisfarne

United Kingdom

OLIVER SMITH St Cuthbert's Way winds through the wild uplands of the English–Scottish border region, following in the footsteps of its namesake early medieval saint. Most sublime of all is its last stage, in which pilgrims must walk across an intertidal zone at low water to reach the Holy Island of Lindisfarne.

Set on England's blustery northeastern shoulder, the tidal island of Lindisfarne has been one of the country's greatest places of pilgrimage for centuries. Most visitors drive here across a 3-mile-long (5km) tidal causeway, taking advantage of the limited hours when the saltwater retreats and a passage to the speck of land briefly opens up. A minority arrive by boat, seeing dunes of marram grass rise from North Sea swells and, perhaps – once Lindisfarne Priory swings into view – remembering the island's history as an early beacon of Christianity in the British Isles.

But the most dedicated pilgrims arrive at Lindisfarne on foot – crossing shoeless from the mainland during low tide, hearing the squawk of seabirds and feeling the squelch of mudflats between their toes, knowing that the sea will soon return and the sacred path will disappear. I made this crossing to Lindisfarne as the final culmination of St Cuthbert's Way – a 62 mile (100km) trail that's perhaps the closest thing modern Britain has to a Camino de Santiago. St Cuthbert is northern England's most revered saint – born in 634 CE, he spent long periods immersed in nature and traversed great distances on foot to spread the word. As Bishop of Lindisfarne he enjoyed time alone in the wild quarters of the island: he felt he could hear God speak most clearly in places of solitude.

The trail that bears his name is a modern creation, plotted to take in places associated with the saint's life – and hikers of religious faith (and none at all) spend days stomping its wildflower-strewn miles, returning to society every evening with soft beds in village pubs. Yet the route passes though some of Britain's most sparsely inhabited corners, and it feels as though the landscapes you cross could have been familiar to Cuthbert himself.

Previous pages: St Cuthbert's Way route threads through superbly scenic Northumberland, here near College Valley. *Left:* Lindisfarne Castle marks the end of St Cuthbert's Way. *Above:* Fishing boats on Lindisfarne's North Sea coast.

DON'T LEAVE WITHOUT ...

1. Exploring Melrose Abbey – an evocative ruin with gargoyles, dragons and saints carved into its medieval masonry.

2. Toasting your walk with a pint in the Ship Inn – the best pub on Lindisfarne – and booking a room for the night to enjoy the atmospheric island without crowds of daytrippers.

3. Visiting 16th-century Lindisfarne Castle, perched imposingly on an outcrop at the island's eastern end, and visible on the horizon during the last stages of St Cuthbert's Way.

Right: Rolling moorland at Coquetdale, in the Cheviot Hills. *Above left:* St Cuthbert's Way starts near Melrose Abbey, where Cuthbert began his religious training. *Above right:* The causeway to Lindisfarne is passable only when the North Sea tides recede.

I started my walk four days earlier in Scotland among the ruins of Melrose Abbey where Cuthbert trained as a young man. Eventually the Cheviot Hills loomed, the path winding over barren moorlands and passing ghostly hillforts and Anglo-Saxon settlements. The England–Scotland border arrived as a fence in a field – but in the quietest and most beautiful parts of St Cuthbert's Way, you sense you might be on another kind of border, between the mundane and the metaphysical, the modern and the mystical.

Cuthbert was also famous for the journeys he undertook in death – after Viking raids in the 9th century, pallbearers carried his sacred bones for seven years to keep them safe. One place where they supposedly hid them was St Cuthbert's Cave – a beautiful overhang set in shadowy forests where hikers find respite from rain and sun.

But, for me, the most stirring episode came on those final miles, where the tidal mudflats were a mirror to the sky: tasting the sea's saltwater tang, and carefully timing the perilous crossing. It's a path that involves planning and invites humility in all who tread it. Here, in one of the most densely inhabited countries in Western Europe, you can find a region of vast horizons, and – in places – some of that same solitude once prized by the saint.

SEEK OUT GORGEOUS WINERIES
AND FARM-TO-TABLE CUISINE

Enjoy wine and fine dining in Valle de Guadalupe

Mexico

SERINA PATEL An emerging wine destination where farm-to-table restaurants and beautiful architecture meet, Valle de Guadalupe is Mexico's top wine-producing region. It's just a two-hour drive south from San Diego, so it's a breeze to dive into its vibrant scene, blessed with year-round hot and sunny days and crisp, clear nights.

To many Southern Californian and Mexican locals, Valle de Guadalupe is a best-kept secret. As well as its beautiful *vinícolas* (wineries), the area is a great place to discover the work of local artisans and enjoy flavorful meals that make the most of local ingredients and fresh Baja seafood. The valley is one to watch and rivals the busier – and pricier – Californian wine regions of Sonoma and Napa.

I like to visit for both weekend stays and day trips, either driving in from California or simply walking across the San Diego–Mexico border via pedestrian immigration. Selecting which wineries to visit is always my hardest task, with more than 150 spread across some 38 sq miles (98 sq km). Many utilize incredible amounts of recycled and sustainable materials; my personal favorites include Bruma, El Cielo, Bodegas Magoni and Decantos Vinícola. Sometimes I go at my own pace, picking two or three locations to visit in a day; if I don't feel like driving, I'll book a guided tour that takes in several vineyards and includes a stop for lunch.

But to fully immerse yourself and relax into the Valle de Guadalupe lifestyle, it's best to stay a night or two. I'd recommend Hotel Andana or Bruma, which promise beautiful nights tucked under a sky of bright stars and lulled by a gentle breeze. A typical day might start with a breakfast of fresh *chilaquiles* (tortilla chips simmered in salsa and topped with cheese) or *migas* (strips of tortilla with eggs), followed by a wine tasting, lunch at a restaurant overlooking breathtaking valley views, and then one or two additional

Previous pages: Valle de Guadalupe's restaurants offer gourmet dining, local wines and fine views. *Left:* Bruma Winery's tasting room. *Right:* Seaside cocktails in laid-back Popotla. *Below:* The valley's 150-plus vineyards offer tours and tasting experiences.

DOMECQ

winery visits. It ends with dinner – from affordable tasting menus and casual bites to fresh seafood and vegetarian options, all paired with delicious local wines. Don't-miss dining options include Fauna (named one of the World's 50 Best Restaurants in 2024) or one of the region's five Michelin-starred restaurants. Many places – such as the revered Animalón – often open for specific seasons, such as summer or autumn, so I make sure to double-check hours and make dinner reservations ahead of time.

On my first visit to Valle de Guadalupe with friends, we spent hours at Bodegas Magoni, hiding from the hot afternoon sun under their beautiful 200-year-old oak tree. We followed with lunch and a wine tasting at Decantos Vinícola; they use a natural gravity-flow process instead of machinery, and it's a picturesque property with large outdoor tables and music. The day ended with enjoying dinner at Malva, which included an unforgettable dessert of corn crème brûlée.

Valle de Guadalupe left me mesmerized and I keep going back, leaving with an exciting list of new wineries, restaurants and accommodations to try out next time. This is more than a refreshingly unpretentious wine destination – it's an experience influenced by creativity, nature and a strong sense of place, where innovation sits side by side with tradition and the slower pace urges you to relax and savor each moment, glass of wine and delicious meal.

Left main: Sustainable chic at Bruma Winery.
Left inset: Valle de Guadalupe's wineries produce a fine array of moreish reds, whites and rosés.
Above: The bar at Hotel Andana, one of the valley's many alluring accommodation options.

DON'T LEAVE WITHOUT ...

1. Visiting the valley's Museo de la Vid y el Vino, where displays showcase the region's winemaking processes and also feature local art.

2. Spending a night at one of Valle de Guadalupe's many architecturally vibrant and serene accommodations.

3. Grabbing a quick bite at Popotla fishing village, for a down-to-earth dining experience.

Hotel-hop South Beach

Miami, USA

REBECCA WALLWORK Florida-hot when everywhere else in the US is not. Cool in an unapologetic, look-at-me way. South Beach is equal parts ritzy city and laid-back beach town – all in one compact, walkable grid. There's no place quite like it for fun in the sun and nights at its glorious art deco hotels – keep your camera ready.

Set against white sands and the aquamarine waters of the Atlantic Ocean, the art deco hotels of South Beach's Collins Ave are an iconic sight. This isn't the gaudier neon-lit strip of Ocean Drive, however, but a more refined cluster of luxury boutique hotels – the newest iterations of the impossibly hip establishments that defined the flashy South Beach scene of the 1990s.

Some of those legendary landmarks are being refreshed for a new era – the Delano is back, and the Raleigh is on the way. Once known for their minimalist designs, glitzy guests and raucous pool scenes, these iconic brands are now serving more of a quiet luxury. Their lobbies exude warmth, with neutral aesthetics that create a feeling of calm – not always easy to find in the heart of South Beach. Even better: you don't have to stay overnight to experience it – a good old-fashioned multi-hotel barhop will do.

What excites me most about the rebirth of this Collins Ave hotel stretch is the chance to relive some of the '90s magic with an evening crawl from lobby to lobby, indulging in the updated cocktail scene along the way. The Delano's beloved Rose Bar has returned, and it's a fantastic place to kick off (or end) your night with a glass of bubbles or a classic cocktail. From there, I like to stroll up to the Shelborne By Proper, to bask in the spacious, high-ceilinged lobby and sip on a South Beach Spritz as I take in the night's live jazz or DJ set.

Also nearby is the new James Miami Beach, a fresh take on the historic Nautilus hotel; and a revamped SLS South Beach. These, along with the Setai and the W South Beach, all offer stylish pit stops for a drink or a see-and-be-seen restaurant for a splashy dinner.

Further south, and a block west on Washington Ave, is another sceney spot worth checking out (and *into*, if you're

Previous pages, left to right: Tala Beach at Hotel South Beach; Sea views from 1 Hotel South Beach. *Left:* Poolside at The Shelborne. *Below:* Photogenic, ready-to-party ambience reigns at the Goodtime, inside and out.

DON'T LEAVE WITHOUT ...

1. Relaxing in South Pointe Park, the perfect location for a picnic of Joe's Stone Crab takeout and a cocktail from Smith & Wollensky's outdoor bar.

2. Grabbing a croqueta or empanada: try the walk-up *ventanita* windows at Las Olas Cafe on 6th St or the Valero gas station on 23rd St.

3. Running, walking or biking the Miami Beach Boardwalk, which extends 7 miles (11km) along the shoreline from South Pointe to Surfside, passing South Beach's hottest hotels.

Below left: The Standard Spa's candy-striped cafe. *Below:* Rooftop elegance at the 1 Hotel South Beach. *Right:* Delightful small plates served up at the 1 Hotel's Drift lobby bar.

on a budget and don't mind cute, compact rooms). With its pastels-and-palms interiors by designer Ken Fulk, and the distinction of being created by musician Pharrell Williams and local nightclub entrepreneur David Grutman, the goodtime hotel is an always-ready-to-party Instagram dream.

For something more serene, step into the soothing lobbies of the literary-leaning Betsy Hotel or the 1 Hotel South Beach, with its eco-conscious vibes. You'll also want to pop over to Belle Isle, where the Standard Spa, Miami Beach welcomes as many Miamians as it does visitors. This is my favorite spot for a sunset catch-up with friends – the Lido deck along Biscayne Bay is a breezy, chic yet relaxed perch for savoring a frosé and petting the locals' cute dogs.

Speaking of adorable creatures, if you're coming to South Beach with kids in tow, I always recommend staying at Loews Miami Beach – for its convenient location, children's club, family-friendly amenities and the way it allows moms and dads to still enjoy what everyone comes to Miami for – a little South Beach glam.

RETRACE NAPOLÉON'S FOOTSTEPS THROUGH WILD PROVENCE

Road-trip through history on the Route Napoléon

France

CHRISSIE MCCLATCHIE A mythical drive through perfumed coastal villages, lavender-scented plateaus and cinematic alpine scenery, the Route Napoléon follows the exiled emperor's legendary 1815 march through the Côte d'Azur and Provence to the French Alps. Where world history, dramatic landscapes and little-known destinations converge, this is a journey best enjoyed in the slow lane.

'It's got to be here somewhere,' I yell back to my husband and two kids as I determinedly push through a tangle of garrigue shrubs at the base of a mountain. I'm using online maps, but the mobile network high up on this vast plateau overlooking the Mediterranean Sea is weak. After a couple of wrong turns, we come across a ruin that, if we use our imaginations, could once have been the Bastide de Broundet. Today, however, this once noble residence is little more than an overgrown jumble of stones.

We're in Séranon, a scattered hamlet of 500 people in the lesser-known upland interior of the Alpes-Maritimes *département*, in France's Provence-Alpes-Côte d'Azur region, where the coastline's blue and gold hues are replaced by a cooler palette of green and browns. The site I'm searching for probably marks the most important moment in Séranon's history: the night Napoléon Bonaparte came to stay as a guest of a local aristocrat. It was March 2, 1815, and the second night of Napoléon's historic march back to Paris after fleeing exile on the Italian island of Elba. He had landed back on French soil the day before at Golfe-Juan, a fishing village tucked between Cannes and Antibes. Over the following days, he marched from the French Riviera to Grenoble, at the edge of the French Alps. From there, he continued on and retook the throne in Paris on March 20th. With power briefly back in his grasp, a tumultuous period known as the Hundred Days followed, before defeat at Waterloo on June 18th ended his rule once and for all.

The route he carved out between Golfe-Juan and Grenoble is today celebrated as the Route Napoléon. As it wends from the sea to the mountains, it passes through a trio

Previous pages: Detour off Route Napoléon to the aquamarine playground of Gorges du Verdon. *Above left:* Discover dairy delights en route in Castellane. *Above:* Grenoble, a key staging post in Napoleon's epic journey to Paris. *Right:* Sample renowned rosés at Provence wineries such as Domaine De Métifiot.

DON'T LEAVE WITHOUT ...

1. Pausing to immerse yourself in the world capital of fragrance, Grasse. Get behind-the-scenes insight into the distilling process at Parfumerie Fragonard, or blend your own scent at Molinard Parfums.

2. Visiting the home of Alexandra David-Néel in Digne-les-Bains, now a museum tracing her adventures and full of fascinating mementos from her trailblazing travels.

3. Climbing the narrow parapet of the Citadelle of Sisteron to admire the route that Napoléon covered on horseback across the Vallée de la Durance.

of distinct landscapes: the sparkling Riviera glamour of the Côte d'Azur; the dry, lavender-fragranced plains of Provence; and the dramatic mountain silhouettes of the foothills of the Alps.

I've driven the Route Napoléon many times over the 18 years I've lived in France, including by motorbike – the classic form of transport for this trip. Recently, I've tried to seek out the tokens of the emperor's passage along the way – whether that's where he slept in Séranon, the bench where he reportedly sat in Saint-Vallier de Thiey (the first village you reach once the perfumed terraces of Grasse are long behind you) or the bridge that he crossed triumphantly in Sisteron, the approximate halfway point of the trail, knowing that he was now assured onward passage towards Grenoble and, ultimately, Paris.

At some 200 miles (322km) long, the route can be completed in a day, but I recommend slowing down and pausing in places like Digne-les-Bains to learn about a lesser-known influential figure of French history, Alexandra David-Néel, the first European woman to set foot inside Lhasa, Tibet. From postcard-pretty Castellane, you may even want to detour into the Gorges du Verdon, France's answer to the Grand Canyon. All in all, this is one of the country's most epic road trips – so buckle up and savor every mile.

Far left: Hill-cradled Castellane. jumping-off point for excursions to Gorges du Verdon. *Left:* France's 'Capital of the Alps', and with a historic center stuffed with museums and galleries. Grenoble makes a fitting end to a journey along the Route Napoléon

GET UP CLOSE
WITH CHIMPANZEES

Take a safari trek in Gombe National Park

Tanzania

ANTHONY HAM Way back in 1960, a young Jane Goodall set out for Gombe in western Tanzania to study chimpanzees. One of the world's most beloved conservationists, Goodall passed away in 2025, and I can think of no better way to honor her work and celebrate her life than to follow in her footsteps.

The first 15 years that Jane Goodall spent with Gombe's chimps were groundbreaking. This was no study from a distance. The primatologist realized that to understand these animals – with whom we share more than 99% of our DNA – she had to get close. Really close. Her approach revolutionized the ways in which animals are studied, and yielded remarkable insights into chimpanzee behavior – how they use tools, kill and go to war with other chimps, form lifelong family (and sometimes monogamous) relationships, and even adopt orphans. More than 65 years after it began, Goodall's work continues, making it the longest unbroken study of animal behavior on Earth.

Whenever I travel to western Tanzania, it feels like a special opportunity to connect with one of conservation's most heartwarming stories. Today's chimps of Gombe are the descendants of those who Goodall knew personally. And they are every bit as accessible as their ancestors were.

My quest begins as I meet my guide, soon after entering the park. Some of the guides here are the children or grandchildren of those lucky rangers who worked with Goodall all those years ago. Those who met her in person love nothing better than to reminisce about their time together.

Beginning my walk is always an exciting moment, as I try to imagine what lies ahead. In this magical world of dense rainforest, unfamiliar sounds swirl around me. Along the forest trails, everything seems alive, soundtracked by the chirrups of insects and the calls of birds and primates. Sometimes the guide remains silent, letting this mysterious place wash over me. At other times, they tell me stories of the chimpanzees and their world – anecdotes about Goodall's time here, the threats faced by Gombe's chimpanzees, and how the park's 100-plus chimp population belong to an endangered subspecies.

Previous pages: Family life in Gombe National Park. *Left:* More than 100 chimpanzees inhabit Gombe's dense rainforests. *Above:* The late Jane Goodall observing Gombe chimps in 2014; her work here revealed valuable insights into chimpanzee behavior.

DON'T LEAVE WITHOUT ...

1. Asking guides to show you Jane Goodall's old chimp-feeding station – no longer in use, but another point of connection to her time here.

2. Walking down to the beaches of Lake Tanganyika, the world's second-largest freshwater lake by volume; that's the Democratic Republic of the Congo just across the water.

3. Visiting the Livingstone Memorial Museum in Ujiji, one of Africa's oldest market villages.

Right: Gombe's forested hills tumble down to Lake Tanganyika's sandy shores. *Above left:* Endless horizons at Tanganyika, the world's second-largest freshwater lake. *Above right:* Gombe treks are soundtracked by waterfalls and the calls of exotic birds.

All of a sudden, the guide stops, hand raised. Everyone falls silent, intensely aware of their surroundings, desperate for that first glimpse. And there they are.

Chimpanzees are gregarious and argumentative, and I never fail to wonder how I didn't see them sooner. Whether in the branches or on the ground, chimpanzee families are always on the move – you might see an individual using a reed to fish termites out of a hole, a mother grooming her baby, an argument between two teenage males. There are times when the resemblance to human beings is uncanny.

The park authorities decree that visitors must stay 32ft (10m) away from the chimps, but try telling that to them. Because these are wild animals, I never quite know how my allocated hour with them will pan out. Sometimes they are utterly unfazed by my presence, which makes it possible to observe them just as Jane Goodall did. On other occasions, they are as curious about me as I am about them – that's when they get really close.

And if my permitted 60 minutes seem like too little time, I always remind myself that there are few finer hours I could possibly pass in nature than the time I've just spent with Jane Goodall's chimps.

TAKE A RIDE
ON THE TOY TRAIN

Ride the Darjeeling Himalayan Railway

India

CHARUKESI RAMADURAI It might seem unusual that tourists in the hill town of Darjeeling on eastern India clamor to sign up for a train ride that takes two hours to traverse just 14km (8.6 miles). But on the Darjeeling Himalayan Railway – fondly known as the 'Toy Train' – the journey is the whole point.

If there's one thing that locals in Darjeeling take for granted, it's the familiar sight of this little blue train winding through the surrounding hills and valleys, tunnels and tea gardens. Along with the Kalka-Shimla Railway up in the foothills of the Himalaya and the Nilgiri Mountain Railway down south in Tamil Nadu, the Darjeeling Himalayan Railway is inscribed on UNESCO's World Heritage list, which designates these lines as 'living examples of the engineering enterprise of the late 19th and early 20th centuries.'

Built by the British to carry precious tea from upland plantations to factories in the big coastal cities (and thereon back to the U.K.), Darjeeling's 'Toy Train' made the first journey along its narrow-gauge mountain tracks in 1881; over time, tea-plantation workers and other locals also used it to travel between the hills and the plains. Tea is transported through quicker and easier means today, but the train continues to thrill tourists (both domestic and from around the world) with its quaint blue coaches and puffing steam engines.

These days, diesel locos power the line's seven-hour, 55-mile (88km) route between Darjeeling and the major rail hub of New Jalpaiguri, but many don't have a day to devote to this longer journey. After exploring Darjeeling's gentle, fog-wreathed sights, I boarded a steam train for the 'joyride' to Ghum, India's highest railway station at 7410ft (2258m). It takes just 20 minutes or so to get from Darjeeling to Ghum by taxi, but the Toy Train takes its time, completing its

Previous pages: A 'Toy Train' approaching the serpentine Batasia Loop. *Left:* Darjeeling's Tibetan Refugee Self-Help Centre wreathed in mist. *Right:* Glenburn Tea Estate now houses a boutique hotel. *Below:* Preparing locally grown teas for a tasting session at Glenburn.

round-trip route in around two hours. Keep your camera ready to capture the Batasia Loop, where the train completes a dizzying 360-degree turn. And on days when the swirling upland mists evaporate, you can catch spectacular views of Khangchendzonga (the world's third-highest mountain) from this spot.

But if you're not pressed for time, the journey from Darjeeling to New Jalpaiguri is entirely worth it. The train chugs slowly through varied landscapes, from scented pine forests to sprawling emerald tea gardens where workers tote baskets of freshly plucked leaves. The route is also bookended by crowded urban streets, with the tracks threading through tightly packed markets where the shops are close enough to reach out and touch through the train window. And everywhere, daily life unfolds outside: kids holding hands on their way to school, chai sellers with their scorched kettles and clinking glasses. Inside the coaches, families and groups of friends share snacks and perhaps break into choruses of popular Bollywood songs to pass the time.

Darjeeling Himalayan Railway tickets sell out early, so buy them in advance through Indian Railways' IRCTC booking portal (use a VPN if booking from outside India). You won't regret it – trundling through the misty green hills aboard the Toy Train is one of India's most memorable experiences.

Left main: Heady mountain views near Darjeeling. *Left inset:* The flower-bedecked veranda at Glenburn Tea Estate. *Above:* Stoking the engine with coals aboard one of the Darjeeling Himalayan Railway's steam-powered trains.

DON'T LEAVE WITHOUT ...

1. Staying overnight at Glenburn Tea Estate; this charming boutique property in the hills around Darjeeling also offers factory tours and tea-tasting, and sells fine Darjeeling teas.

2. Visiting Darjeeling's Tibetan Refugee Self-Help Centre, to learn about the complex political history of India's Tibetan community and pick up authentic souvenirs.

3. Alighting at Ghum Station for a peek at the tiny but fascinating museum showcasing the history of the Darjeeling Himalayan Railway.

ENCOUNTER A TRADITIONAL PACIFIC SOCIETY

Experience Fa'a Samoa

Samoa

CRAIG MCLACHLAN With an over-quota of white-sand beaches, turquoise waters and swaying palms, Samoa easily satisfies standard images of a South Pacific paradise – but it also displays heartwarming pride in its unique Polynesian culture. Despite the best efforts of missionaries and foreign powers, Samoa and its people have clung to Fa'a Samoa – the cherished 'Samoan Way'.

At 8:45am on every morning of the working week, the 30-member Royal Samoan Police Band marches from the police station in Samoa's capital, Apia, to raise the country's flag outside the Government Building at 9am. I love this authentic must-see. The band plays and accompanying officers march with unbridled enthusiasm and national pride – it's Fa'a Samoa on full display.

While daily life here may seem casual and relaxed, beneath the surface there's a complex code of traditional etiquette that is rigorously upheld and means everything to locals. *'Aiga* (extended families) are at the heart of Fa'a Samoa – this is a 'we' society. The goal of traditionally minded Samoans is to serve, strengthen and improve the prospects of their *'aiga*. Each is headed by a *matai*, who represents the family; there are 362 villages in Samoa and some 1800 *matai*. Respect for elders is crucial and children are expected to obey not just their relatives, but all the adults in their village. Christian values, brought to the island in the 1800s, have been seamlessly integrated – every village has at least one sizable church (a source of local pride, and ideally larger than those in neighboring villages); almost everyone attends on Sundays, dressed up in their formal best.

While a visit to Apia's Samoan Cultural Village introduces aspects of culture and traditional life – such as weaving, traditional *tatau* (tattoo), dance and lunch from an *umu* (hot-stone oven) – the best way to see Fa'a Samoa in action is to get out among the villages. My favorite way to do this is by staying in a *fale* – a thatched-roofed wooden platform, traditionally with woven blinds for walls – on the beaches of southeast 'Upolu, the main island. I also enjoy strolling the two-hour trail around the nation's third-largest island, peaceful Manono, where the four villages are home to just 800 people. It's only a 20-minute taxi-boat ride off 'Upolu's

Previous pages, left to right: *Fale* at Lalomanu, 'Upolu; Samoan pineapples. *Left:* Taking pride in meticulous maintence of local churches, such as Apia's dazzling cathedral, is integral to Fa'a Samoa. *Below:* The snazzy Methodist church in Matafele, Apia.

DON'T LEAVE WITHOUT ...

1. Swimming in outrageously photogenic To Sua Ocean Trench, a giant sinkhole with sheer, green-draped rock walls; it's accessed by a precipitous (but sturdy) wooden ladder.

2. Shopping for anything and everything at Apia's vibrant Fugalei Market, an obligatory social experience, enlivened by the colorful chaos of the adjacent bus station.

3. Cooling off with a dip at lovely Togitogiga Waterfalls in O Le Pupu-Pu'e National Park near 'Upolu's southern coast.

Below left: Dipping in to the turquoise waters of To Sua Ocean Trench is an essential Samoa experience. *Below:* Fa'a Samoa in full flow as fire-dancers perform at a traditional *fiafia* event. *Right:* Find fresh Samoan produce and a whole lot more at Fugalei Market in Apia.

western tip, but it's like a different world, with no roads, cars or canines – a place where older kids are happy on big-wave days when boats can't take them to high school on the mainland. Another wonderful window into Fa'a Samoa is attending a *fiafia* (happy get-together) night, involving dancing, singing, music and cooking; the villagers who perform in the shows are equally as enthusiastic as the visitors enthralled by the spectacle.

Most of Samoa's stunning outdoor attractions are on land owned by local villages. I'm happy to fork out the small fee to clamber down into spectacular To Sua Ocean Trench, to swim in the pristine cool waters of Piula Cave Pool or snorkel out into the Savaia Giant Clam Sanctuary. My contribution benefits local people: in Savaia, the funds are used to beautify the waterfront village and enhance facilities at the local school. Sanctuary caretakers collect fees and watch over gear while visitors are out snorkeling, enjoying close-up views of the massive, colorful bivalves of which Savaia is so proud.

With Fa'a Samoa as its cornerstone, this is a proud Pacific country; it's also a captivating place to visit.

A FRESH PERSPECTIVE
ON GREEK HISTORY

Dive into an unexpected underwater world

Greece

DEEPA LAKSHMIN Greece's islands and peninsulas are an ideal gateway to the Aegean Sea and what lies beneath its surface: adventurous wreck- and cave-diving that's rooted in centuries of marine exploration. Just as Athens' Acropolis honors the ancient Greeks' legacy, each coastline tells its own story about the people and the aquatic life who call this place home.

I thought I knew what the color 'deep blue' looked like – and then I learned to scuba dive. Vibrant coral reefs convinced me to get my open water certification, and like many divers (and snorkelers), I planned ocean time around tropical sites famous for colorful ecosystems. Show me the rainbow!

But Greece seduced me with rich shades of cobalt, indigo, sapphire and turquoise, all melting together as I descended to witness what so few humans have the privilege to see in the wild: a curious octopus reaching out a tentacle; flounder, flat and camouflaged, disappearing into sand; starfish clinging on for dear life; spiky, venomous lionfish (an invasive species in the Mediterranean) pestering native populations. Greece's underwater world teemed with life, just as its islands do.

In Chania, Crete, I plunged 33ft (10m) with local legend Papakastrisios Spiros, who discovered many of the island's dive sites by swimming the coastline. Spiros is now in his 60s, and alongside his his extended family, he runs the no-frills Blue Adventures dive shop to train the next generation of scuba explorers – myself included. The day after completing my PADI advanced open water course, I followed him through an underwater tunnel, holding hands with my dive buddy on my first-ever cave dive. My fear turned to exhilaration when we surfaced among stalactites and stalagmites – limestone formations millions of years in the making, lit only by our flashlights. This was Elephant Cave, named after the fossilized elephant bones scattered about. How did they get here, I wondered, so far from their African and Asian counterparts? This place was also once their home – or rather, their prehistoric ancestors'

Previous pages: Fish rule Crete's underwater realm. *Above left:* The author coming up for air after exploring the *Mitilini* wreck near Halkidiki. *Above:* Down deep in Elephant Cave. *Right:* A perfect porthole frame while wreck-diving the *Panagis*, off the Athens' islet of Fleves.

DON'T LEAVE WITHOUT ...

1. Contributing to a citizen science project. I focused on seagrass conservation off Souda Beach, but do some research and pick what's most exciting to you.

2. Eating real Greek yogurt – this daily breakfast gave me energy for back-to-back dives without making my stomach turn inside out on the boat.

3. Watching the sun set over Cape Sounion's Temple of Poseidon, dedicated to the ancient Greeks' god of the sea – the perfect way to end a dive trip.

home, long before land and sea divided into the continents we know today.

As my 10-day trip continued, I was often reminded that I was a mere guest in the underwater world. Swimming over the *Mitilini* and *Panagis* wrecks – cargo ships that fought the waves and failed, and now lie offshore of Halkidiki near Thessaloniki and Athens' islet of Fleves – I felt like a tourist visiting not just another country but a parallel realm, where everything constructed by humans has been reimagined as part of the ocean floor. Schools of fish darted through an algae-covered boat propeller and fireworms, thick like furry caterpillars, dotted sunken bows.

Then there's the endemic seagrass that absorbs carbon, protects baby fish and nurtures microscopic organisms with macroscopic impact. Officially it's called *Posidonia oceanica* or the Grass of Poseidon, but locals also call it the 'lung of the Mediterranean' because it replenishes oxygen in an environment that desperately needs more of it.

Now, swaying in the current somewhere off Plakias, there are pieces of growing seagrass that I planted – my way of saying thank-you for letting me visit. I came to Greece knowing how to dive, and I left understanding why we dive.

Far left: Climb up to the Temple of Poseidon to see the sun set over the Greek god's domain. *Left:* The author gained her PADI advanced open water certification in Chania, opening a window into an astonishing underwater world.

Marvel at Monteverde's cloud forest

Costa Rica

SARAH GILBERT Monteverde's tropical cloud forest is an environment unlike any other. Wrapped in ethereal wisps of mist, echoing with birdsong and – literally – dripping with life, this primordial world is a magical multisensory experience, a chance to disconnect from the urban jungle and discover untamed nature.

It was just after sunrise and the cloud-forest soundtrack was a chorus of chirrups, caws, whistles, whoops and trills. Squelching along the mist-wreathed trails, I stopped to admire feathery ferns and lofty trees cocooned in moss, branches draped with bromeliads. Above me, a keel-billed toucan perched like a flamboyant flower, its outsized rainbow-colored bill quizzically tilted. It was impossible not to smile.

Monteverde (meaning 'green mountain') sits high on Costa Rica's mountainous spine, where moist air from the Caribbean collides with dry air from the Pacific – so creating a biodiversity hot spot. Thanks to rising temperatures and deforestation, cloud forests around the globe are shrinking, but Monteverde's history is rooted in conservation.

It was settled by Quaker dairy farmers in the 1950s, who joined forces with environmental organizations and the local community to create the pioneering Reserva Biológica Bosque Nuboso Monteverde (Monteverde Cloud Forest Biological Reserve) in 1972. Today, the region is an evergreen patchwork of protected land, and its profusion of flora and fauna is as awe-inspiring as the communal commitment to preserving it.

Whether you're an avian expert, a budding birdwatcher or don't know your tanager from your trogon, the birding in Monteverde is epic. Around 400 species pass through at one time or another, and enlisting the help of a naturalist guide (try Pasión Costa Rica) will help you spot them. Evocatively named hummingbirds – violet sabrewings, green-crowned brilliants, coppery-headed emeralds – hover excitedly around feeders at Café Colibri at the reserve's entrance, with an audible buzz from their tiny wings as they beat at around 70 times a second.

Previous pages: Monteverde's lush cloud forest. *Left:* The resplendent quetzal is one of Monteverde's many brightly colored bird species. *Above:* From the forest floor to the vines supporting epiphytic bromeliads, every inch of this misty wilderness supports life.

DON'T LEAVE WITHOUT ...

1. Booking an adrenaline-fueled adventure at Selvatura Park – whizzing over the cloud forest on its state-of-the-art zipline or strolling along its 2-mile (3km) Treetop Walkway.

2. Signing up for a sustainability tour at Valle Escondido; El Pueblo's bean-to-cup coffee tour; or Santuario Ecológico's Costa Rican cooking class.

3. Enjoying a farm-to-fork feast, from Valle Escondido's brick-oven pizza to organic fine-dining at Hotel Belmar at the San Lucas Treetop Dining Experience.

Right: Hummingbirds gather around sugar-water feeders at Café Colibri, near Monteverde's entrance. *Above left:* Crossing a rope bridge on a trek through the forest. *Above right:* Starting the day right at a Monteverde lodge before a birdwatching excursion.

But Monteverde's most famous feathered resident is the aptly named resplendent quetzal. I was about to give up on a sighting of this spectacular species – sacred to the Aztecs and the Maya, and on every birder's bucket list – when I came across not one but three. Two young males, dazzling in their shimmering green plumage, scarlet bellies, fauxhawks and flowing tail feathers, squabbling over a much plainer female.

For another side of the forest, I took a night walk in the Reserva Curi-Cancha, a private reserve with trails that wind through primary, secondary and open forest. Enveloped in an inky blackness, I listened out for magnified nocturnal noises – chirping crickets, croaking frogs, rustling foliage.

My guide's flashlight picked out the enormous eyes of a kinkajou – an intriguing cross between a monkey and a small bear. And what I thought was a shadow transformed into a somnolent three-toed sloth, curled up in a tree fork. I marveled at a diminutive glass frog, its translucent belly revealing its tiny beating heart, and sidestepped a venomous side-striped palm-pit viper coiled by the side of the path, which made my heart beat that bit faster.

Before I left, a shaft of moonlight revealed a sleeping toucan, its long bill resting on its back, inquisitive eyes closed until sunlight dappled the forest again.

SEE STARS AND SHIPS

FROM A RHODE ISLAND LIGHTHOUSE

Turn temporary keeper at Rose Island Lighthouse

Rhode Island, USA

PIA PETERSON HAGGARTY Growing up in Rhode Island, I loved to visit Newport's cobblestone streets and reveled in the summer tourist buzz. Today, the city's music festivals and Gilded Age mansions are no secret – but few know that nearby in Narragansett Bay, you can play keeper for the night at one of the state's iconic lighthouses.

Crowning an 18-acre (7-hectare) island in Narragansett Bay, between Newport and Jamestown, the Rose Island Lighthouse was built in 1870 as an essential guide for shipping in the bay. It was rendered obsolete in 1969 when navigation aids were installed on the newly opened Newport Bridge, and the buildings fell into disrepair. Determined not to lose such a historical treasure and pristine green space to vandalism or private use, a group of committed local citizens came together to save the lighthouse, working to repair the buildings and preserve the land.

Today, the efforts of the original campaigners – including co-founder of the Rose Island Lighthouse Foundation Charlotte Johnson – are continued by a nonprofit organization, seasonal staffers and volunteers. The island is open and accessible not only to the local and migratory birds who claim refuge in what's now a wildlife sanctuary, but to the visiting public – including overnight 'keepers' who (between the months of April and October) can pay to stay in the restored buildings. The lighthouse now functions as a museum during the day, but in lieu of having a keeper to staff the site overnight, the foundation invites members of the public to book stays in the lighthouse and foghorn buildings, as well as in barracks that date to the late 18th century.

With solar-powered electricity, no wi-fi and rainwater cisterns providing the water, staying here is an almost completely off-grid experience that truly calls to mind the island's historical

Previous page: Rose Island stays allow a detox from modern life. *Left:* A crewman on the Jamestown-Newport Ferry, which runs between the three islands. *Right:* A replica of the fresnel lens in the lighthouse tower. *Below:* A view of Rose Island shows the rocky out-cropping of the island.

heyday at the turn of the 20th century. Nowhere in the state will you have a better view of the bay than from the top of the light tower, from where you can watch sunrises and sunsets, and check out the incredibly intricate Fresnel lens up close (the one in place today is a replica of the original).

There's a working kitchen and grills for overnight guests to use, but as there are no restaurants or stores you'll need to pack food for your stay (or a picnic if you visit as a day-tripper) – I picked up corn muffins to grill for breakfast at Jamestown's East Ferry Deli. Spend your time on Rose Island contemplating the water or walking along the beach; thanks to the currents swirling around the bay, the shoreline is rich in washed-up shells, sea glass and driftwood. When I visited, we also swam from the beach or right off the ferry dock (boat arrivals permitting); on Tuesday evenings and Sunday afternoons you can watch the J-22 sailboat races around the bay. The buildings also host residencies for Rhode Island artists, and you might catch temporary exhibitions that reveal different perspectives of the landscape here.

During the bird nesting season (March 1 to August 15), parts of the island are closed off, but you can still roast marshmallows over the fire pit, play games on the lawn and relax in the Adirondack chairs to take in the beauty of this small part of New England.

Left: Diving off the boat dock in the summer in Narragansett Bay. *Above:* The interior of an overnight room in the Fort Hamilton Barracks.

DON'T LEAVE WITHOUT ...

1. Scouring the shores not only for sea glass and whelks, but also seagull skulls which often are picked clean by fish and wash back up on the island.

2. Walking around the catwalk at the top of the lighthouse, to enjoy 360-degree views of the bay.

3. Breathing in fresh sea air during the ride aboard the Jamestown–Newport Ferry or the *Rose*, the official passenger boat of the island.

KAZAKHSTAN'S CAPITAL DAZZLES

WITH FUTURISTIC ARCHITECTURE

Admire Astana's architecture

Kazakhstan

ANNA KAMINSKI Rising from the steppe like some modernistic mirage of glass and steel, Kazakhstan's bold, fast-growing capital is the legacy of the country's forward-looking former president, Nursultan Nazarbayev. Its monumental boulevards, giant chrome spheres and megastructures shaped like yurts and pyramids are an architectural reflection of Astana's goal to become Central Asia's most technologically advanced city.

Millennia-old ram- and deer-shaped gold pendants, crafted by ancient tribes that once roamed the Eurasian steppe, glittered inside the National Museum of the Republic of Kazakhstan. Elsewhere within the striking glass-and-stone building, anthropomorphic sculptures, bronze vessels, weaponry and ceramics found in burial mounds spoke of centuries of human civilization. It took me a couple of hours to take it all in, and to admire the light-filled entry hall with a golden eagle soaring above a map of the country.

Across the street lies the Palace of Peace and Reconciliation, Norman Foster's 203ft-high (62m) glass, granite and steel pyramid symbolizing the peaceful coexistence between the different religions and cultures of Kazakhstan. The obligatory tour revealed the soaring atrium and its model of 2030s Astana, but the highlight for me was the plant-hung Winter Garden at the pyramid's tip, with stained-glass works by British artist Brian Clarke.

Nursultan Nazarbayev's vision of Astana as the forward-looking 21st-century capital of Kazakhstan shone through when I strolled showpiece street Nurzhol Bulvar, designed by renowned Japanese architect Kisho Kurokawa. This 2-mile-long (3km) symbolic 'Bright Path' took me from the Ak Orda (presidential offices) to the Khan Shatyr shopping mall; shaped like a crooked yurt (or perhaps a wizard's hat), its heat-absorbing exterior maintains summer temperatures inside even in the depths of winter. En route, I was particularly taken with the golden-green towers of Parliament, the giant egg housing the National Archive, the sinuous Northern Lights skyscraper trio – and the Bayterek Monument, a latticed tower topped with a glass orb, inspired by the Kazakh legend in which mythical bird Samruk lays a golden egg containing the secrets of happiness beyond human reach.

I found Nur Alem – housed inside a vast gleaming sphere resembling Darth Vader's Death Star – even more visually

Previous pages, left to right: Pack a picnic to admire Astana's skyline from the Ishim River. *Left:* Inside Nur Alem, now home to future-focused displays. *Below:* The Bayterek monument and observation tower was completed in 2002.

DON'T LEAVE WITHOUT ...

1. Eating at Qazaq Gourmet, sampling modern spins on traditional Kazakh dishes – such as lamb braised in camel milk – served to the sounds of an electric *dombra* (traditional string instrument).

2. Shopping at Khan Shatyr, the yurt-shaped shopping mall designed by Norman Foster; upstairs there's a beach club with pool and sandy 'shore'.

3. Ascending the 318ft-high (97m) Bayterek Monument for fantastic views of Nurzhol Bulvar, and to place your hand over former president Nazarbayev's golden handprint.

Below left: The Ak Orda (presidential office) is framed by Astana's Nurzhol Bulvar, the city's showpiece 'Bright Path'. *Below:* Chef Artem Kantsev explains a dish at Qazaq Gourmet. *Right:* Designed by Norman Foster, the translucent, tentlike Khan Shatyr is another Nurzhol Bulvar architectural marvel.

arresting. Designed by Adrian Smith + Gordon Gill Architecture for Astana's 2017 Expo, it now houses Kazakhstan's most ambitious museum, devoted to renewable energy. After playing with interactive, multilingual displays on space energy, hydroelectric projects and solar power, I was genuinely surprised and inspired by many of the solutions to global energy problems, from Bionic Power wearable tech to the water-power-harnessing GreenWave. The crowning touch? The sustainable and environmentally efficient vision of Astana in 2050 on the top floor.

Not all of the capital's showstopping contemporary architecture looks uber-futuristic. My last stop was the Astana Grand Mosque – Central Asia's largest – which opened in 2022 and can accommodate some 230,000 worshippers. I was struck by how its design – by the UAE's Dewan Architects – is firmly rooted in Kazakhstan's centuries-old Islamic heritage, with specific nods to national culture. Rooted in tradition, yet wholeheartedly embracing the future, Astana feels like a city that is truly coming into its own – and the time to visit it is now.

ETHICAL MARINE-WILDLIFE TOURISM

Embark on ocean adventures

French Polynesia

JESSICA LOCKHART Does it feel a bit obvious that we're suggesting a tropical South Pacific destination for its aquamarine waters? Fair enough. But in French Polynesia, ocean adventures aren't limited to flopping on white-sand beaches – they're an opportunity to gain deeper insight into the Polynesian culture and way of life.

In 2024, French Polynesia – a semi-autonomous French territory – was thrust into the spotlight when the powerful break at Teahupo'o played host to the Paris Summer Olympics' surfing competitions. Yet, a more significant event took place that year with much less fanfare. Along with Indigenous leaders from New Zealand, Tonga, the Cook Islands and Hawai'i, officials from French Polynesia signed He Whakaputanga Moana – a declaration recognizing whales as legal persons with inherent rights.

Every year around July, humpback whales arrive in French Polynesia's balmy waters to give birth and nurse their young. Their coming doesn't just signal the start of tourism season – it has significant cultural ties. For thousands of years, the animals' movement has been used as a marker of time. In Polynesian culture, whales are seen as guardians or ancestors; sacred creatures to be revered.

This deeply held respect is reflected in how tourism has been developed here to best interact with – and protect – marine wildlife. Widely considered one of the best whale-watching destinations for those who want to have an ethical encounter, French Polynesia has strict industry regulations, which were further tightened in 2025. Only when the conditions and behavior of whales align just-so can a small group of swimmers slip into the water to observe the graceful giants from a safe and respectful distance. And on World Ocean Day in 2026, French Polynesia expanded its marine sanctuary – already the world's largest – even further.

Most visitors flock to Tahiti, Bora Bora or Mo'orea for whale-watching. I, however, flew to the tiny island of Rurutu. This raised coral atoll

Previous pages, left to right: Accommodation on stilts in Bora Bora; surfing breaks. *Above left:* Humpback whales nurture their calves in the ocean around these islands. *Above:* Rurutu, a tiny atoll where whales can be viewed from the shore. *Right:* A crab picks through flotsam on a low-lying *motu* (coral atoll) islet.

DON'T LEAVE WITHOUT ...

1. Diving at the 'Wall of Sharks' in the Tuamotu Archipelago, where huge numbers of gray reef sharks congregate to form a 'wall' in the currents at the South Pass of Fakarava Atoll.

2. Admiring how iridescent Tahitian black pearls – one of the country's top exports – are cultivated at Love Here Pearl Farm on Taha'a.

3. Learning to surf – another deeply spiritual Polynesian practice – at the black-sand beach of Papeno'o on the island of Tahiti.

lacks a shallow lagoon, which allows whales to swim so close to land that they're visible from shore. By the time I arrived in late October, the whales had already begun journeying south to their Antarctic feeding grounds – yet I didn't miss their absence. There were so many other ways to discover the links between Polynesian culture and the ocean – like gliding across the waters of Baie de Matavai off the coast of Tahiti in a *va'a* (outrigger canoe). As the saltwater splashed around me, I considered how ancient Polynesian wayfarers must have felt sailing across vast oceans in these *va'a*, using only the stars, birds and waves as their guides.

Of course, there are also more contemporary ties – like overwater bungalows, said to have been pioneered in French Polynesia during the 1960s and inspired by traditional fishers' huts. From the bathtub of my bungalow at Le Taha'a by Pearl Resorts, I could gaze down and see colorful fish and reef sharks swimming directly below. I wasn't on my honeymoon, but all the same, I was in love.

To be an island nation means learning to live with the constant rhythm of the ocean and its inhabitants. To be French Polynesia means finding new ways to protect and admire one of the world's most valuable resources.

Far left: Emerald peaks roll down to overwater accommodations on Mo'orea Island, another top whale-watching destination. *Left:* Visiting Love Here Pearl Farm on Taha'a offers fascinating insight into the islands' famed Tahitian black pearls.

DISCOVER AFRICA'S

TROPICAL SECRET

Discover Africa's unsung island paradise

São Tomé & Príncipe

ANTHONY HAM São Tomé and Príncipe is one of Africa's more closely held secrets. The nation's two main islands are covered in forests and fringed with islet-studded bays and deserted beaches, and its soulful stories revolve around dramatic geological landforms, Portuguese-influenced architecture and fabulous food and music. I was hooked from the moment I arrived.

Let's start with some basics. Rising abruptly from the middle of the ocean, São Tomé lies 190 miles (306km) west of Gabon's coast, while Príncipe is 246 miles (396km) from Equatorial Guinea's shores – and nearly 100 miles (160km) of open ocean separates the main island of São Tomé from smaller Príncipe. United in one country, São Tomé and Príncipe (STP to its friends) offers quiet and gentle pleasures for the most part. It's the kind of place where I spend my days exploring forest trails and beautiful beaches under a balmy tropical sun; and where my nights consist of dining on fresh local seafood and then falling asleep to a soundtrack of waves lapping on the shore. When I wake up the next morning, repeat. I realized pretty quickly during my first visit that life here is very close to how I imagine it really should be lived.

Stretching just 30 miles (48km) north to south, and 20 miles (32km) east to west, São Tomé packs a lot into quite a small area. In the south, the wonderful 2175ft-high (663m) Cão Grande rises above the forest, a bizarre finger of volcanic rock. The further you travel, the more such protrusions you'll find, poking above the forest like monuments to some petrified lost civilization. In places, the forest is slowly reclaiming ancient haciendas of Portuguese plantations – haunting reminders of the harrowing years of colonial rule.

My perfect São Tomé day begins with a hike into the forest from the tiny village of Santa Josefina – passing the 890ft-high (271m) rock tower of Cão Pequeno, and continuing along the shoreline of Rio do Portinho until I arrive at the tiny, deliciously isolated cove-beach of Praia de Santo António Mussacamú, inaccessible by any road.

Over on little Príncipe (which covers just 55 sq miles/142 sq km), the sense of isolation clings to places of staggering beauty. The Baía das Agulhas (Bay of Spires) lives up to

Previous pages: São Tomé Town, this island nation's compact capital. *Left:* Paradise found at pristine Praia Banana, one of Príncipe's many ravishing beaches. *Above:* Don't miss sampling just-caught seafood, grilled at roadside stalls in São Tomé Town.

DON'T LEAVE WITHOUT ...

1. Sampling fresh seafood and Portuguese-influenced dishes from roadside stalls and sit-down restaurants – Ecolodge Mucumbli or Restaurante Celvas on São Tomé's northern coast are standout choices.

2. Hiking through the forest amid otherworldly rock formations to the little-known beach of Praia de Santo António Mussacamú.

3. Watching whales and taking a scenic helicopter ride at Príncipe's Baía das Agulhas (Bay of Spires).

Right: Cruising quiet palm-lined roads on São Tomé. *Above left:* Cão Grande rises above the Rio Caué in forest-cloaked southern São Tomé. *Above right:* São Tomé's Ecolodge Mucumbli serves delectable seafood as well as Portuguese-influenced cuisine.

its name, with a forest of granite outcrops – it remains one of the most beautiful panoramas I have ever seen over a lifetime spent traveling the African continent. Jump in a helicopter for a scenic flight – or go whale-watching, swim with sea turtles or snorkel the pristine waters. And speaking of pristine – a much-overused cliché that actually undersells the transparency of Príncipe's waters – the island's beaches effortlessly project that 'lost paradise' feel.

Two beaches among many stand out for me. From your first sighting of Praia Banana from the clifftop, your day is all about deep forest greens and golden sands between a cobalt sky and ocean. No wonder Bacardi shot their classic ad here many years ago – it's still an icon in the industry for the perfect tropical escape.

The ad execs could just as easily have chosen Praia Boi, my own personal favorite and another stretch of white sand you can only reach by walking along a forest trail, serenaded by birdsong as you go.

SEE THE WORLD
FROM A NEW PERSPECTIVE

Flightsee in the 'Last Frontier'

Alaska, USA

REGIS ST LOUIS Discover why Alaska is known as the 'Last Frontier' while soaring above a wilderness of glaciers, forests and mountains. The USA's largest state is also its most rugged, with a mere 20% of its territory accessible by road. There's no better way to experience this awe-inspiring northern realm than on a scenic flight.

From afar the hills appear dotted with white boulders. As we draw closer, I soon realize these pale stones are actually mountain goats. They stare up with a look of mild curiosity as our helicopter passes slowly over the mountain valley. I spot more than a dozen of them before losing count, as the pilot pipes in 'We saw 26 on the first trip over today' before redirecting my gaze to the vast frozen river stretching out below us. 'That's the Bear Glacier, the largest in the Kenai Fjords.' In fact, this behemoth stretches for some 12 miles (20km) from its head up near the vast Harding Icefield to its terminus at the edge of Resurrection Bay, just south of Seward.

Even more dazzling than the glacier are the floating icebergs in all shapes and sizes, which glimmer like jewels on the mirror-like blue-green waters surrounding them. Out of the helicopter's right window I spot a small group of kayakers paddling amid these floating sculptures. From this lofty vantage point, the world below is reduced to a realm of pure shape and color. The green on the mountains is tufted velvet; alpine lakes amid the snow-dotted peaks are an electric blue of Caribbean intensity.

We skim along the coast, passing several other sinuous glaciers before turning back inland to face the soaring peaks looming above the shoreline. Temperate rainforest lines the valleys in an impenetrable carpet of evergreen. Moments later I spy craggy granite summits rising above wide snowfields clinging to the slopes; in a heartbeat, we enter an alpine landscape

Previous pages: Glaciers shaped Denali National Park. *Left:* A wild stretch of shoreline on the edge of Kenai Fjords National Park. *Right:* Helicopter flight over Bear Glacier Lagoon, part of Kenai Fjords National Park. *Below:* Mountains meet the sea in the view across Resurrection Bay near Kenai Fjords National Park.

unseen by most visitors to this rarefied corner of the state.

Few other places in the world are so well suited to flightseeing as Alaska. One of Anchorage's top attractions is Lake Hood, home to the busiest seaplane base on the planet. Watching them roar across the water and soar off to remote corners, you can feel the pulse of excitement – although being on board is a different magnitude of exhilaration.

On the Kenai Peninsula, I'd felt the adrenaline rush as we traveled over mountains, forests and glaciers on just one short excursion. Elsewhere, you can circle North America's highest peak while gliding over the sprawling wilderness of Denali National Park. Further south, you can fly in a bush plane to watch massive brown bears feasting on salmon at Brooks Falls in Katmai National Park. And why not combine flightseeing with outdoor adventures – going dog-sledding after landing atop the Harding Icefield, or kayaking through a glacial lagoon followed by an aerial overview.

Scenic flights here aren't cheap – but nor are they forgettable. After my own flight, I stuck around the landing pad and watched as a family climbed out of a helicopter. They had wide grins as they looked at one another, trying to put words to the near spiritual experience they'd just shared. 'We will always remember this day,' Tirth, a software engineer living in Seattle, said to me. 'It was the trip of a lifetime!'

I couldn't agree more.

Left main: A snowy mountain range in Alaska. *Left inset:* Flying through a mountain valley in Kenai Fjords National Park. *Above:* View over Seward, a town that sits at the head of a mountain-backed deep-water fjord in south-central Alaska.

DON'T LEAVE WITHOUT ...

1. Taking a hike: walk to a glacier overlook in Kenai Fjords National Park, or make the more challenging ascent to the Harding Icefield.

2. Getting on the water – kayak through a glacial lagoon with Liquid Adventures or book a wildlife-watching cruise with Major Marine Tours, both based in Seward.

3. Feasting on fresh seafood – a meal of wild Alaskan salmon, tender halibut, hearty seafood chowder or decadent king crab legs is the perfect way to celebrate your adventures.

DISCOVER OTHERWORLDLY

WATERY BEAUTY

Be wowed by wonderful Killary Fjord

Ireland

DANIEL BOLGER On the Wild Atlantic Way in the west of Ireland, hidden along the intricate coastline and down the track-like roads of Connemara, Killary Fjord is a strong contender for the most breathtaking, achingly beautiful place in the country – and folks, let me tell you, that is saying something.

Mountains rise and fall across Connemara's remote landscape and beautiful beaches dot its shores – but no sight compares to the singularly majestic Killary Fjord. I moved to Ireland in 2006 and in all that time, I've never been as genuinely overawed as when I first visited Killary, said to be the country's only true fjord. It cuts its way 10 miles (16km) inland towards the village of Leenaun (or Leenane), past steep peaks shining luminous green in the summer and glowing burnt auburn in autumn and winter.

This place is so visually arresting that I didn't know at first what to do with the experience. But a quiet peace came upon me on the banks of the harbor; I guess you could call it meditation. As a visitor, it's a slower pace here. Tranquil. The landscape doesn't ask anything except that you respect it, imparting a feeling that you have no place to be that's better than where you are; nothing much more pressing than deciding what to eat later on.

You'll need your own wheels to explore Connemara and visit the fjord. It's only a 40-minute drive from Westport (County Mayo) and Clifden (County Galway), but it's well worth staying here to explore the surrounding scenic treasures – Leenane Hotel or the lovely old-world Renvyle House nearby are both good bets. Leenaun's village (with its cozy pubs) and harbor are embraced by mountains, including Mweelrea, the Devil's Mother and Maamturks, so you'll be spoiled for hikes. Or take a trip with Killary Fjord Boat Tours, which brings you through the harbor and past studded mussel farms and unique views (keep eyes peeled for dolphins), with the area's scenery, geography and history explained along the way. From Killary Adventure Centre, you can power through the fjord on a kayak or SUP, or partake in archery, coasteering, gorge walking, high-ropes courses and an obstacle course through the Connemara bog. Head northeast of

Previous pages, left to right: Shoreside views over Killary Fjord and its smattering of mussel farms; Aasleagh Falls. *Left:* The fine swath of sand at Glassilaun Beach lies within easy distance of Killary Fjord. *Below:* Pearly dunes meet calm blue waters at Glassilaun.

DON'T LEAVE WITHOUT ...

1. Trying the famed Killary mussels somewhere along your journey through West Connemara, best accompanied by fries and a Guinness. A perfect meal.

2. Checking out one of the pretty nearby beaches – Silver Strand to the north and Glassilaun to the south are my favorites (note that parking is limited).

3. Taking part in the locally organized Connemara Mountain Walking Festival, held in spring and offering immersive, local-expert-guided hill-walking excursions in the region.

Below left: Blooming rhododendrons offset Killary Fjord's deep blue waters. *Below:* Fresh Killary mussels are cooked up in pubs and restaurants across Connemara, and go down a treat with a pint of Guinness. *Right:* Killary is stunning from all angles, whether driving shoreside, on foot or heading out onto the water.

the village to the pretty Aasleagh Falls, and you might be lucky enough to see salmon leaping or otters skulking.

But if you do only one thing on your visit to this criminally undersung destination, make it hiking the darkly named but sensorially astonishing Famine Walk. This 11-mile (18km) route tracks along the side of a mountain through the fjord, from Bunowen to the pier at Rosroe, and loops back along an inland road – but Killary is worth seeing twice, so stay on the fjord and go back the way you came (around 4 miles/7km each way). You'll pass grazing sheep and the sparse, haunting ruins of a 19th-century village, Foher, whose inhabitants all died or emigrated during the Great Famine; you can still see the rolling imprints of the 'lazy beds' (furrows for growing potatoes) that once sustained them. To reach the trailhead, park at the gravel storage area near Tullyconnor Bridge on the N59, about 4 miles (6km) west of Leenaun, and walk down the road signposted Bunowen.

So pack your rain gear and some sturdy shoes and get yourself to Connemara – like now.

ENCOUNTER REVITALIZED

COMMUNITIES AND COASTLINE

Trek the Michinoku Coastal Trail

Japan

LISA WYNNE In the north of Honshū, Japan's main island, the beautiful and storied Tōhoku region is often missed by international tourists – but with epic scenery, rich culture and charming hospitality, it's a worthy place to visit. Tracing Tōhoku's Pacific edge along the Michinoku Coastal Trail, my hike here was paved with warm welcomes and dramatic natural beauty.

When I think of long walking trails, I envision immersing myself in nature – but in northern Honshū, it is nature's furious power that's long had a hand in shaping the beautiful scenery. The coastal communities here are sustained by the bounty of the Pacific Ocean, but are also at the mercy of its changing moods. Though I saw frequent reminders of the devastating 2011 tsunami during my Michinoku Coastal Trail hike, I also encountered many people focused on reconstruction and revitalization of the impacted areas. Developed as part of post-disaster recovery efforts, the Michinoku Coastal Trail is special particularly because of this dialogue between people and landscape along its 600-mile-plus (1000km) length. It's an invitation to the world to come and see how locals and nature rebound.

The trail's northern terminus is the picture-postcard shrine of Kabushima in Hachinohe, Aomori Prefecture; the route spans four prefectures, ending just beyond the Miyagi border, and takes in both urban roads and national parks. As a designated walking trail, it's mostly a paved or dirt-track, but there are more challenging sections.

In Miyagi Prefecture, I visited the spacious seaside Natori Trail Center, a hub for through-hikers and section-walkers. Run by the non-profit Michinoku Trail Club, it has practical amenities like showers, a shop and a lounge, plus an enormous 1:55,000-scale wall-map of the entire route. The staff are friendly, experienced hikers and local experts, and I received great advice and recommendations, such as tips for bear-safety as a solo walker.

I started at Miyako in Iwate Prefecture and ended at Hachinohe in Aomori – a distance

Previous pages, left to right: The sea from the woods along the trail in the Tanesashi Coast area; Rhyolite stones, made from volcanic rock, on Jōdogahama Beach. *Above left:* The Michinoku Coastal Trail island-hops to unique Tashirojima, where cats vastly outnumber humans. *Above:* Jōdogahama Visitor Center. *Right:* Take a break from the trail to enjoy fine dining aboard the Tōhoku Emotion train between Hachinohe and Kuji.

DON'T LEAVE WITHOUT ...

1. Retracing your hike route between Hachinohe and Kuji aboard the Tōhoku Emotion restaurant train, to reflect on your adventure in luxurious cars serving local food and drink in a fine-dining atmosphere.

2. Stamping your Trail Passport (available online or at Natori Trail Center), a personalizable souvenir and great icebreaker as you collect stamps along the way.

3. Island-hopping near Ishinomaki – the trail traverses Tashirojima and Ajishima, and sacred Kinkasan off the Oshika Peninsula. Check ferry schedules in advance.

of 148 miles (238km). JR trains, the charming Sanriku Railway Rias Line and local buses run more or less parallel to the trail, so I could join up the most interesting sections. From larger towns along the route, rail services also connect inland to the Tōhoku Shinkansen mainline direct to Tokyo.

One day on the trail could include windswept beaches, quiet forests, cliff paths and rural roads lined with rice fields. While there are many camping facilities en route, I recommend staying at inns, lodges and guesthouses. This supports the local economy, and I loved meeting the charming, knowledgeable hosts and experiencing warm baths and relaxing hospitality after long days outside. When booking, I chose overnight rates including dinner and breakfast so I could enjoy local seafood and specialty dishes, and feel rested and recharged for the next big day's walking.

Whether embarking on a full thru-hike, or planning sections into a wider itinerary across Japan, the Michinoku Coastal Trail is a rewarding and often deeply moving adventure. In a region marked by tragedy and dotted with memorials, I found so much to learn from its resilient communities, and tremendous joy and delight to be found in the beauty of its coastline.

Far left: Hikers brave the elements below the Kitayamazaki Cliffs on the Michinoku Coastal Trail. *Left:* The Michinoku Trail Club issue hiking passports, which can be stamped at points along the route to mark the progress of each walker's hike.

DANCE THROUGH THE CITY

WHERE TANGO WAS BORN

Dance sultry tango in Buenos Aires

Argentina

ISABEL ALBISTON Argentina's frenetic capital is a pulsing, passionate city where, each day, couples and strangers alike come together in a sensual embrace to dance tango. Watching this celebrated genre in its hometown Buenos Aires can be spellbinding, but trying it yourself is an even bigger thrill. So skip the touristy shows and join locals on the dance floor.

There is nothing quite like dancing tango in Buenos Aires. It brings a feeling of connection, presence and shared experience as you move with your partner to the music, intuiting their next move through their touch as you glide around other couples. The city offers a packed schedule of *milongas* (tango dance events), held at various locations on different days. Each has its own vibe, from traditional salons hosting afternoon *milongas* to more informal gatherings and Tango Queer events, where people of all genders dance with whomever they like.

In Palermo, La Viruta is a long-standing venue that attracts a mix of novices and experienced dancers. Nights here begin with a class, and there are usually performances by tango orchestras. La Glorieta is an open-air *milonga* held at a pretty park bandstand in the Belgrano neighborhood – I challenge you to find a more romantic place for a date. But my favorite *milonga* is La Catedral, a low-lit, rustic hangar-like space in Almagro with mismatched furniture and a huge heart above the bar. The live music is excellent and the bohemian atmosphere unique; sometimes cats wander casually across the dance floor.

It took me a while to get the hang of tango etiquette at an Argentine *milonga*. Certainly, the person leading should have enough skill to avoid colliding with other couples. Between tangos, people sit at tables around the dance floor, sipping drinks and keeping careful watch for a *cabeceo,* another dancer's nod of the head and held gaze which serves as an invitation to dance. This non-verbal cue is not without its dangers: I once leapt to my feet in excitement before realizing the nod was for a woman seated behind me.

For a sense of history, head to a *milonga* in San Telmo. It was here (as well as in the neighboring port district of La Boca) that tango music emerged in Argentina during the

Previous pages: Tango dancers at La Glorieta *milonga* in the city's Belgrano district. *Left:* BA from above, with the grand Palacio del Congreso in the foreground. *Above:* Beloved tango singer Carlos Gardel is commemorated by a mural near his namesake museum.

DON'T LEAVE WITHOUT ...

1. Visiting the Museo Casa Carlos Gardel, set in the former home of tango singer Gardel, where you can listen to his melancholic lyrics, often steeped in longing for a far-off homeland.

2. Shopping for tango shoes at Comme Il Faut, an exquisite Recoleta shop selling women's dancing shoes designed and manufactured in Buenos Aires.

3. Hearing an *orquesta tipica* (tango orchestra), an ensemble of musicians that usually includes someone playing a *bandoneón* (a type of accordion).

Right: Tableside tango at a restaurant along El Caminito, in the La Boca district. *Above left:* Diners at a restaurant within Buenos Aires' vast Mercado de San Telmo. *Above right:* Tango is an artful expression of the city's sensuous passion.

late 19th century, at the same time as it was first played in Uruguay. In San Telmo, the once grand mansions of the Buenos Aires elite had become tenement housing for impoverished European immigrants and people with a mix of South American and African heritages. As I walk through its atmospheric cobbled streets today, I like to imagine musicians gathering in the buildings' shared courtyards on sticky summer nights to play the instruments of their respective homelands, blending musical styles and African candombe beats to create a new genre known as tango. These days, dancers perform for tips at Plaza Dorrego during the San Telmo Sunday street fair.

But you don't have to search too hard to encounter tango in Buenos Aires. When I lived on Avenida Boedo, I once opened my front door on a Saturday afternoon to find a stage set up in the street and the Orquesta del Tango de Buenos Aires preparing to perform. As they played, a local couple began to dance on the pavement. Watching them, the city's very essence seemed to be expressed through the tango.

ETHEREAL ARTWORK
IN AN ANCIENT LANDSCAPE

Immerse yourself in art in the Red Centre

Australia

JESSICA LOCKHART Australia's outback is often characterized as a flat, barren place – but while it may be isolated, central Australia is anything but empty. The landscape constantly shifts the longer you look at it, revealing beauty and vibrant life to those willing to give it the time – or to capture it on canvas.

I sit beside Anna Dakin, an artist and the owner of Art Tours of Australia, as she spreads out cakes of paint and jars of water on a picnic blanket around us. We're at Simpsons Gap in the Northern Territory – a scene that's been captured by countless Australian artists, including famed Aboriginal landscape painter Albert Namatjira.

After a tutorial on technique, it's time to put brush to paper. Around us, the sandstone cliffs framing the waterhole transform from punchy shades of orange to deep hues of red. As the day's heat eases, birds begin calling to one another from above. From between the rocks, black-footed wallabies suddenly materialize, as though from a liminal ether. It's a place that's certainly not lifeless and desolate.

Since the 1970s, when dot paintings first began appearing in international art galleries, central Australia – an area with roughly defined boundaries stretching from Uluṟu-Kata Tjuṯa National Park to Alice Springs – has been globally celebrated as a hotbed for creativity. Its relative isolation has played a role in the development of artforms seen nowhere else in the world, with the landscape serving as the central character. Colorful parrots, serene waterholes and ancient mountain ranges are frequently depicted in paintings, weavings and pottery emerging from the region. But a rock isn't just a rock here; art often tells stories from the Dreamtime – an ancestral space that shapes people's connection to the natural world.

Previous pages: The red-rock monoliths of Kata Tjuṯa. *Left:* Heady views at Kings Canyon. Nearby is Bruce Munro's Light-Towers installation. *Right:* Alice Springs' Iltja Ntjarra (Many Hands) Art Centre. *Below:* Alice Springs, long a Red Centre creative hub.

In Alice Springs, artists keep the region's traditions alive at studios such as Iltja Ntjarra (Many Hands) Art Centre, where visitors can watch the descendants of Albert Namatjira hone their craft. For 30 years, this is where a group of Western Arrarnta artists have been decorating pots with imagery that speaks to their cultural beliefs, traditions and values.

But like the landscape, Central Australian art isn't homogenous. It, too, continues to shift, change and evolve, with multidisciplinary national and international artists using lasers, drones and sound installations to tell their stories. Further south at Uluṟu-Kata Tjuṯa National Park, I settle in for a picnic featuring Indigenous bush tucker ingredients like smoked emu and kangaroo. The day gives way to night and suddenly, 1100 drones whir above and start painting pictures in the sky, telling just one chapter of an ancient Mala story. The show is called Wintjiri Wiṟu, which translates to 'beautiful view out to the horizon' in the local Aṉangu language. It joins Bruce Munro's *Field of Light* – a landscape of 50,000 glowing spheres at the base of Uluṟu – as one of Ayers Rock Resort's signature art experiences. But my favorite is *Sunrise Journeys*, a newer dawn experience, where the artwork and music of four Aṉangu artists is projected onto the surrounding trees and sand. As the sun breaks over the horizon, I feel like I have a better understanding of how the environment is seen through Aṉangu eyes. All around me, everything is alive.

Left main: Simpsons Gap has inspired generations of artists, including famed landscape painter Albert Namatjira. *Left inset:* A work in progress at Iltja Ntjarra (Many Hands) Art Centre. *Above:* A magical drone-designed dance of light, Wintjiri Wiṟu tells a chapter of an ancestral Mala story.

DON'T LEAVE WITHOUT ...

1. Participating in Art Tours of Australia's outdoor watercolor painting workshops.

2. Wandering through *Light-Towers* at Kings Canyon, the Red Centre's latest installation by Bruce Munro. Spread across the desert, the 69 towers change color and emit lovely music.

3. Attending April's Parrtjima, a 10-night contemporary art festival just outside Alice Springs that uses light and technology to reimagine ancient stories.

THE ULTIMATE ISLANDS
FOR NATURE AND WILDLIFE

Go on a Galápagos expedition cruise

Ecuador

SANDIE KESTELL Sitting some 600 miles (965km) off the coast of mainland Ecuador, the isolated Galápagos Islands number among the best wildlife-watching destinations on Earth. Forever linked with Darwin and the theory of evolution, here you'll find an astonishing variety of landscapes and wildlife, many endemic to these lands, seas and skies.

The Galápagos are made up of 13 main islands plus dozens of smaller islands and islets, stretching over some 23,000 sq miles (59,500 sq km) of the eastern Pacific Ocean. That's a lot of water and ground to cover, and the remoteness of the outer islands makes them inaccessible to independent travelers. Yet these are sometimes the only places to spot certain wildlife – so if you want to see everything (or as much as possible) that the Galápagos has to offer, I'd recommend an expedition cruise with an experienced operator like National Geographic-Lindblad. Seeing the Galápagos by boat opens up the archipelago greatly, including (itinerary permitting) opportunities to visit the outlying islands.

A typical day aboard ship can include up to four excursions, often with two or even three options for each. The itinerary might begin with a pre-breakfast outing at around 6:30am. The second excursion follows after breakfast, with one or two more activities in the afternoon. In between, the ship is usually repositioning to the next point of interest while you're refueling, changing clothes or catching a lecture with an onboard guide or naturalist.

Deciding which excursions to do is the toughest part of a trip like this. Here's an example: anchored at Tagus Cove off Isla Isabela in the western part of the archipelago, I had a choice between epic scenery and lava flows on a hike to Lake Darwin, set in a tuff cone on the slopes of Volcán Darwin; taking a Zodiac ride along the coast searching for Galápagos penguins and other birdlife; or kayaking the same area for wildlife viewing. Though I was keen on hiking in Darwin's historic footsteps and I love a nice paddle, ultimately I couldn't risk missing a penguin sighting – and I wanted to be hands-free to take photos at a moment's notice. Watching these cute little penguins waddling on the rocky shore and diving into the deep was one of the highlights of my entire trip.

Previous pages, left to right: Sally Lightfoot crabs add a dash of color to Galápagos shorelines; Endemic Galápagos scalesia trees. *Left:* Dragon Hill overlooks the northwest coast of Isla Santa Cruz. *Below:* Flower-filled backstreets in Puerto Ayora.

DON'T LEAVE WITHOUT ...

1. Visiting El Manzanillo Ranch in the highlands of Isla Santa Cruz for the chance to see dozens of giant tortoises in the wild.

2. Deep-water snorkeling off the coast of Isla Fernandina to spot green sea turtles, Galápagos sea lions, marine iguanas and all kinds of fish.

3. Hiking the 370-plus steps to the summit of Mars-like Isla Bartolomé to gaze across at Pinnacle Rock and Isla Santiago.

Below left: Volcanic landscapes abound in the Galápagos, such as these fumaroles at Volcán Chico on Isla Isabela. *Below:* Channeled into the Santa Cruz coast, Las Grietas is a popular swimming spot. *Right:* Snorkel the coastline to see green sea turtles and other wildlife, from manta rays to marine iguanas.

At least half of the cruise expeditions are experienced under water; you'll have plenty of opportunities to deep-water snorkel, sometimes twice a day. Depending on where you are, you'll be mesmerized by green sea turtles, marine iguanas, frolicking sea lions, Galápagos penguins, giant manta rays, sharks and an incredible variety of fish. Be sure to give the wildlife plenty of distance – at least 6ft (2m) – and follow the lead of your naturalist guide.

Almost every itinerary takes in Puerto Ayora on Isla Santa Cruz, home to the Charles Darwin Research Station. At this breeding center for giant tortoises, you can learn about research and conservation projects, and see baby and juvenile giants. Inland, at El Manzanillo Ranch, there's also the chance to watch giant tortoises in the wild as they slowly graze on grass and bathe in ponds. Listen closely – there's something extraordinary about hearing these slow-moving, prehistoric-looking reptiles inhale and exhale.

This is as 'Galápagos' as it gets – but then you could easily say the same after every encounter with nature and wildlife in this extraordinary place.

VARIED CUISINE

AND STAR-RATED CITIES

Follow a foodie trail

Taiwan

PIERA CHEN Sixteen Indigenous tribes, waves of migration from China and 50 years of Japanese rule have given Taiwan a versatile culinary repertoire. This is enhanced by fresh seafood and a terroir that produces both high-mountain tea and sun-loving mangoes. Thankfully, the island isn't huge – you can go far with a small suitcase and two stomachs. Trust me.

Taiwanese cuisine is intimately tied to the island's history of migration and colonization. It began with the cooking of the Indigenous Austronesians, using hunted, fished and foraged ingredients. This was followed by the thick soups and hearty stir-fries of Hokkien and Hakka communities, who migrated from China in the 16th century. Japanese colonial rule from the late 19th century introduced miso, raw fish and tempura; after WWII, Chinese nationalists retreating to Taiwan brought the culinary customs of Shanghai, Sichuan and Guangdong. The Dutch and Americans also left their mark – Chiayi's *jirou fan* (turkey rice) has roots traceable to Dutch and US servicemen celebrating Thanksgiving. All these influences mingled and evolved like the flavors in *siraw* (the pickled raw pork of the Indigenous Amis people), lending local cuisine a distinct identity.

Tainan, Taiwan's oldest city and former capital, is celebrated for its huge breakfasts. You can graze all morning at Yongle Market, with 200 stalls spilling onto the streets beyond. Try specialties like *wanguo* (a savory rice pudding steamed in a bowl), *renbing* (soft spring rolls) and *cai zong* (rice dumplings with taro). After breakfast, venture out: sample the sweetest scalded squid at Michelin-lauded Yeh Jia Calamari Rice Noodle; stop at Hei Gong Hao for grass-jelly shaved ice heaped with *boba* (tapioca balls); or indulge in a seven-course dinner at 19th-century village residence Zhu Xin Ju, also Michelin-recommended. Many of Taiwan's best-known foods originated in Tainan, and while you can try them elsewhere, the city is where they're at their best – in particular milkfish, which comes braised, pan-fried or in congee; and *wenti niu* ('warm' beef), just-slaughtered local

Previous pages, left to right: Try local specialties at Taiwan's night markets, like oyster omelets at Tainan's Garden Market; Shallots laid out to dry. *Above left:* Appetizers at a roadside banquet (pan-toh; banzhuo) in Kaohsiung. *Above:* Skewers for sale at Dongdamen Night Market in Hualien. *Right:* Passionfruit flowers are a common ingredient in Taiwanese cuisine.

福州世祖
胡椒餅
註冊商標
饒河夜市創始店
俗傳承
$65
米其林餐盤
椒
餅
商
標
福州
世祖

DON'T LEAVE WITHOUT ...

1. Trying local booze: craft beer and tea-infused cocktails at a bar; *gaoliang* (sorghum liquor) from a convenience store; or whisky on a tasting tour at Kavalan Distillery in Yilan.

2. Dining at one of many vegetarian pay-by-weight buffet restaurants (some are Buddhist-run) throughout the island; the overall standard is high.

3. Buying made-in-Taiwan chocolates (Fu Wan is a good brand) to go with your Sun Moon Lake oolong tea or Alishan coffee beans.

beef that's scalded in broth, stir-fried or dipped in hotpot.

Cosmopolitan capital Taipei lays claim to Taiwan's top European kitchens and the best Japanese cuisine outside Japan – not to mention the most Michelin-starred restaurants. Taipei's other culinary specialty of *niurou mian* (beef noodles) were allegedly dreamed up by Sichuan veterans who migrated here after WWII and got creative with chili paste and canned beef rations from the US military. *Xiaolongbao* (pork soup dumplings) are worth trying at least once at the iconic Din Tai Fung – prepare to queue.

Taipei also has its share of riveting markets. I take visitors to Raohe Night Market for pork pepper buns and stinky tofu; and one of my favorite morning exercises is trawling Binjiang Wholesale Fruit and Vegetable Market and the streets beyond for mountain produce. Keelung Night Market is worth a half-day trip northeast of the capital for its seafood selections.

Indigenous cooking is most prevalent on the wild and beautiful east coast. Dishes can range from grilled fish and chrysanthemum greens to hornet larvae, mountain rodents and sea smelt – all washed down with millet wine. Whether you're an adventurous or careful eater, Taiwan's national love of food will reward you generously.

Far left: Preparing pork pepper buns at Raohe Night Market in Taipei. *Left:* Sample the seafood at Keelung Night Market in the far north of Taiwan.

DISCOVER A REMOTE
ITALIAN ARCHIPELAGO

Sail the Aeolian Islands

Sicily

BREKKE FLETCHER I love Italy, and I don't care who knows it. As a repeat visitor to the *Bel Paese* (Beautiful Country), I have always longed to explore its islands and coastlines by sea, to drop anchor and dive off a sailboat. My wish came true last summer on a weeklong sail around Sicily's famous Aeolian Islands.

Dream trips can be risky. What if, after all the planning and investment, the experience you envisioned as being life-altering turns out to be average? But then I encountered the Sailing Collective on Instagram a year ago, and something clicked. As well as private charters, they offer more affordable, set-itinerary group trips, in which you join other guests aboard a six-person (plus two crew) catamaran. I shared a link to an Aeolian Islands sailing with a friend, to check whether she (or more aptly, we) could stomach the idea of sharing tight quarters with strangers for six days and seven nights. She replied: 'Oh yeah, let's do it!'

Doubts dimmed as affirmations about seizing the day bounded around my brain. I held my breath and booked the trip.

My friend and I arrived on a Saturday, to allow for any travel snafus and to explore a scorchingly hot Palermo. Once our city adventures were complete, we hopped on a train to the marina in Capo d'Orlando. After a night at a motel there, we awoke Sunday morning to board our home for the week: the *Sonia*, a Lagoon 46 catamaran.

There we met our fellow passengers, our onboard chef Flannery, and Captain Dayyan, who gave us our safety briefing before we motored northeast (sailing is dependent on the wind). We anchored off the coast of Isla Vulcano for our first swim and shared 'OMG, how is this happening?' moment. Chef Flannery prepared lunch in the ship's tiny galley as we splashed around, overjoyed. Still wet and salty from the sea, we devoured pasta with fresh tomatoes and basil, steamed mussels, prosciutto with melon and glasses of chilled wine.

Then we sailed on, dropping anchor to spend the night at remote Punta del Perciato off Lipari. Apart from one other boat, we were all alone. The sunset took my breath away.

Previous pages: Touring the Aeolians by sailboat is a magical way to see these unique islands. *Left:* Beware the stone stacks between Lipari and Volcano. *Above:* The trip included stopoffs to explore tiny, little-visited Aeolian harbors.

DON'T LEAVE WITHOUT ...

1. Getting on a paddleboard. Even if you can't stand up, you can use it as a makeshift kayak to explore coves and caves.

2. Procuring a fresh catch. Chef Flannery negotiated with a nearby fishing boat (in a bikini, no less) for the tastiest meal of the trip.

3. Talking with locals; you don't need to be fluent in Italian to greet and thank the people you meet while exploring the islands, with a *ciao* and a *grazie*.

Right: Lunchtime aboard the *Sonia*, where delicious meals came courtesy of an onboard chef. *Above left:* The shoreline of Salina, where the party came ashore for dinner at a seaside restaurant. *Above right:* Azure shades in the Aeolian chain.

The next day was more sailing and swimming, and on our second night, we jumped into a dinghy to visit the charming, hilly seaside town of Porto di Panarea for cocktails and dinner.

From Panarea, next stop was Stromboli in search of *granita* (a typical Sicilian frozen dessert). I broke away from the rest of the group to meander the island's narrow paths – finding some alone time was essential for me.

Departing Stromboli, there was a hint of lava with a smoky haze surrounding the summit of the island's active volcano. Onward we sailed to Salina for dinner at a beautiful sea-facing restaurant, Porto Bello – their *spaghetti al fuoco* was as spicy as it was divine.

Our last day saw us sail to Filicudi, my favorite island of the entire trip. We walked ashore to the tiny village of Pecorini a Mare, then sailed to the lighthouse islands of La Canna. The final anchorage was nearly inside a blue grotto – absolutely breathtaking.

The only downside of the trip was that it had to end. But I am not being hyperbolic when I say this experience exceeded my expectations – it was, indeed, a dream trip come true.

A NATIONAL PARK

WITH ALL THAT'S WILD ABOUT BORNEO

Glide on a longboat to orangutan territory

Malaysia

MARCO FERRARESE Borneo has been shaped by rivers for thousands of years – just like its wildlife and Indigenous communities, who have relied on waterways to settle and survive in the once-impenetrable rainforest. Take a longboat across the dark-green Batang Ai Lake and experience it first-hand on the fringes of Batang Ai National Park.

I'm seated in a longboat, looking out at jagged crests bursting with rainforest, their jigsaw ends dipping into a majestic expanse of glistening water. Batang Ai National Park, slung where south-central Sarawak slips into Indonesia's Kalimantan, is breathtaking even if it's the work of humans, not nature.

When this 9-sq-mile (24-sq-km) area was flooded in 1985 to create a hydroelectric dam, the local Iban communities relocated a few miles west to Lubok Antu, the town where civilization ends and water marks the beginning of a wild patch of world. Some of the proud and resilient Iban, whose grandfathers still hunted for human heads to appease their system of animist spirits, stayed behind in Ulu Ai, their ancestral land upriver. This primeval forest is only accessible by meandering for about two hours on a longboat, gliding past peaks and islets across the lake, to the communal longhouses the Iban built to the west of Batang Ai National Park's entrance.

Their only neighbors live up in the trees: the park and its adjoining Lanjak-Entimau Wildlife Sanctuary total about 536 acres (217 hectares) and, according to the Wildlife Conservation Society, hold 80% of Sarawak's estimated 2000 wild orangutans. The most adventurous way to see them is to strike out on the Red Ape Trail, a challenging five-day trek to campsites along the upper reaches of the Delok River.

The hike was developed by Kuching-based tour operator Borneo Adventure, which has worked with Batang Ai's Iban since 1987. They are one of the few agencies able to organize

Previous pages: Borneo's forests are filled with rivers and waterfalls. *Left:* Longboats are moored on Batang Ai's reservoir, ready for adventures upriver. *Right:* Ayam pansuh, chicken cooked in bamboo stalks. *Below:* Communal living in the traditonal Iban longhouse at Nanga Sumpa Lodge.

trips into the national park, as there are no public boats from the Lubok Antu jetty. Those who can't or don't want to spend a week braving jungle trails and oversized creepy crawlies can still chase orangutans by gliding up the Delok in a longboat and trekking for short segments. While ape sightings are certainly not guaranteed, the park's wealth of flora, birds, reptiles and insects always reward the effort getting here.

The best place to stay is Nanga Sumpa Lodge, built by Borneo Adventure on the shore of the Delok River, next to the namesake longhouse. There's no phone reception or internet here, so time moves to the rhythms of sloshing water and a cacophony of insects. The most intrepid can travel a couple of hours upriver to the rustic Lubok Kasai Lodge, deep in orangutan territory, and spend the night by candlelight, waiting to strike out on the trails at daybreak.

All twenty Iban families in the Nanga Sumpa longhouse live in adjacent dwellings – the *ruai*, or common verandah, connects all the doors and acts as a shared working and living space – and welcome guests. Meeting the headman and bonding over a few rounds of the sugary *tuak*, the local rice wine, is a local custom.

I sit on the wooden floor with the headman, downing round after round of the stuff, as Iban women around us chat and laugh while weaving rattan baskets to sell to visitors for an additional income, so that tourism can keep them living here, happy, at the edge of the world.

Left main: A bird's-eye view of Batang Ai's waters, now protected as a national park. *Left inset:* Mending fishing nets in the Iban longhouse at Nanga Sumpa Lodge. *Above:* Casting a net from a longboat on the Delok River near the lodge.

DON'T LEAVE WITHOUT ...

1. Having a traditional Iban meal of *ayam pansuh*, chicken cooked in bamboo stalks filled with water and jungle leaves over a fire.

2. Stopping for a refreshing dip at the Enseluai Waterfall, a natural pool surrounded by wild forest, only reachable by longboat.

3. Visiting the Nanga Sumpa longhouse in the evening and then again in the morning to see how different the Iban lifestyle is during and after working hours.

About the Authors

ANNA KAMINSKI has been a guidebook author for Lonely Planet since 2010, covering destinations as diverse as Kazakhstan, Jamaica, Papua New Guinea, Mongolia, Mexico and Spain. Born in the Soviet Union and raised in the UK, she now calls Andalucia home. When she is not writing about tourism or food, you can find her hiking in the mountains of Axarquia or paddle boarding in the Mediterranean.

ANTHONY HAM has written nearly 200 guidebooks for Lonely Planet. Fluent in Spanish, he lived in Madrid for 10 years, and has for three decades been traveling the globe in search of stories, from all corners of Africa and the Amazon to the heart of Europe. He has written three books of narrative non-fiction, and writes for the *New York Times* as well as other magazines and newspapers around the world.

BAILEY FREEMAN is a culture writer and photographer who loves learning from the world and the people in it. She's authored guidebooks for Lonely Planet and DK Eyewitness, and has written online features for other national and international media including Matador Network, Adventure.com and The Infatuation. Bailey lives in Nashville, where she also works as an aerial acrobat and runs Suspended Gravity Circus. Follow her travels at @the_traveling_b on Instagram.

BECCA HUNT is the Publisher of Lonely Planet's Inspiration & Gift books. She lives in the Bay Area with her husband (a tree photographer) and son (a young travel pro), and they escape to the endless beauty nearby every chance they get.

BREKKE FLETCHER is a food-obsessed traveler, so any trip starts with what and where to eat. Nothing makes her happier than discovering a spot that's not on anyone's radar, meeting the owner, and letting them order for her. She'll always say yes to new adventures, but also loves to do nothing – *il dolce far niente*. Working at Lonely Planet is a dream. Don't wake her up!

CAROLINE TREFLER is a longtime travel writer and editor. She lived in Toronto and Montreal before moving to New York City, but as a true Canadian, she hasn't lost the tendency to say 'sorry' all the time. Some of her favorite adventures have been solo-road-tripping across Canada, camping in Jordan's Wadi Rum desert, swimming with deadly jellyfish in Australia, rock climbing in Thailand, hiking in Patagonia, horseback riding in Central Asia and bicycling in Japan and Taiwan. Track her travels at @carolinetrefler on Instagram.

CHARUKESI RAMADURAI is a freelance journalist writing on travel, wildlife, sustainability and conservation for various publications around the world, including *National Geographic*, *Condé Nast Traveller*, BBC Travel and Nikkei Asia. Her passion for new travel adventures has taken her to over 75 countries across seven continents, covering a wide range of experiences from riding with a traditional eagle hunter in western Mongolia to hiking in the white wastelands of Antarctica. Follow her travels at @charukesi on Instagram.

CHRISSIE MCCLATCHIE swapped Sydney for France in 2007, originally for one summer. She hasn't managed to leave and today calls the village of Villefranche-sur-Mer outside Nice home. She sold wine to superyachts in the Mediterranean and led tours through the vineyards of Provence before embarking on a writing career over a decade ago. She authors Lonely Planet's Côte d'Azur and Monaco titles and is at her happiest reporting stories about France, food and wine, and life by (or on) the water.

CHRISTINE GILBERT is a journalist, travel writer and circus artist who is originally from Houston, Texas. She has authored six Lonely Planet guidebooks. During her nine years in Argentina, she lived in both Buenos Aires and Bariloche – where she wrote about food trends, hopped fences while covering the 2022 World Cup celebrations, and connected with subcultures in everything from escape-room tourism to aerial dance. She enjoys climbing mountains with her husband and drinking a strong *mate*.

CRAIG MCLACHLAN has been writing guidebooks and articles for Lonely Planet for over 25 years. A kiwi with wanderlust, he's a Japan specialist and has written a number of books about his adventures in his wife Yuriko's homeland. He's also worked on guidebooks all around the planet for LP, extensively in Europe and the South Pacific. Craig has an MBA from the University of Hawai'i, where he found it awfully hard to concentrate. craigmclachlan.com

DANIEL BOLGER is Lonely Planet's Destination Editor for Italy & Southeast Europe. He comes from just outside Philadelphia, but came to Dublin in 2006 and never left. When he's not knee-deep in Italy, Greece or Balkans travel writing, he's exploring Dublin and Ireland with his wife, two kids and dog.

DEEPA LAKSHMIN is the Director of Social Media at Lonely Planet and a journalist based in New York City. She's written for *National Geographic*, MTV News and Vox, among others, and has covered everything from travel to entertainment to politics. Born and raised in Pennsylvania, she travels because it reminds her how big and beautiful the world is outside of her comfort zone. See her adventures (and photos of her cat) at @deepa on Instagram.

HARRIET AKINYI OWALLA is an award-winning Kenyan travel journalist whose journey into travel began unexpectedly, thanks to an adventurous aunt who introduced her to the joy of exploring new places. Since then, she's turned that spark into a purpose: to document Africa's beauty, complexity and wonder with honesty and heart. Passionate about representation, Harriet is proud to be part of the growing chorus of African travel writers shaping the continent's global narrative.

ISABEL ALBISTON has been researching and writing Lonely Planet guidebooks for more than 10 years, covering countries in four different continents. Her favorite beat is Argentina, where she lived for five years and still considers her second home. Since moving back to Ireland, she has found her way to South America regularly for adventures in the Andes, stargazing in the Atacama Desert, horseback riding in Uruguay and to dance tango in Buenos Aires. Follow her at @isabel_albiston on Instagram.

JAMES PHAM has visited more than 70 countries as a writer, editor and photographer, and has been living in Southeast Asia for the past 22 years, including Cambodia, Thailand and now Vietnam. When he's not traveling, you can usually find him hitting backhands in the Saigon heat or slurping down a heaping bowl of spicy noodles.

DR JENNY WALKER is a higher education consultant and travel writer. Having worked in Oman for over two decades, she now lives up a mountain in Northern Spain with her husband and hound. Author of an academic book on desert travel literature, published by Routledge, co-author of an off-road book on Oman,and the writer of over 60 chapters for Lonely Planet, she has lived, worked or traveled in 125 countries, from Mexico to Mongolia.

JESSICA LOCKHART is Lonely Planet's Destination Editor for Oceania. She's spent the last decade housesitting across New Zealand and working in Australia as an award-winning journalist and guidebook author, but still has a strong Canadian accent. When she's not writing about tourism and conservation, you can find her hiking, camping, biking or paddling. Find her via jesslockhart.com or @WynneLockhart on Instagram.

JOEL BALSAM is a freelance journalist who has contributed to more than a dozen Lonely Planet guidebooks, including chapters on Québec and New Mexico. He was born and raised in Canada, where he spent over a decade living in Montréal. He has since moved to Rio de Janeiro, Brazil, where he loves dressing up in silly outfits for Carnaval. Find him at your nearest market, tasting fruit and street meat. Find him via joelbalsam.com or @joelbalsam on Instagram.

JULIA BUCKLEY is a journalist and author based between Venice and Sicily. She's spent the past five years exploring the Veneto region from mountain top to beachy bottom, with apologies to her ancestors from Genoa, Venice's historic rival. A former travel editor for UK newspapers, she's contributed to Lonely Planet guides to Italy, as well as writing about the Bel Paese for other US, UK and Italian publications.

JULIE F KING leaves most every place she visits researching the local real estate ads, enamored of my imagined new life there. Whether it's Copenhagen or Lewisburg, WV or Deer Isle, ME, she finds herself captivated by the peculiarities of place that capture the local spirit. That being said, she just cannot quit her current and beloved hometown, Baltimore, MD. Come sit with her. She'll tell you where to eat and what to see.

LISA WYNNE is an avid reader, writer and hillwalking member of Mountaineering Ireland. She spent half her twenties living in Yamagata, Japan, before circumnavigating the globe with Japanese NGO Peace Boat, then heading home to Dublin, Ireland. She has worked in education, sustainable tourism, fashion, and public service, but is most at home in the mountains. Her favorite things include textiles, unique ice-cream flavors, and the grand stretch of Irish summer evenings. lwynne.com

LUCIE GRACE is a British Maltese writer who has lived in Thailand for five years and has enthused about the 'Land of Smiles' for Lonely Planet, The Daily Beast, *National Geographic Traveler* and numerous other magazines and newspapers. She has visited 60-plus countries and is the co-author of eight Lonely Planet titles including India, South India, Croatia and the Balkans, as well as writing two books for Hoxton Mini Press: *Britain's Best Saunas* and *Music London*.

MARCO FERRARESE has been living in Penang, Malaysia for well over a decade, where he travels and covers Southeast Asia, South Asia and beyond for some of the most renowned international guidebooks and publications. In the footsteps of fellow countryman and namesake Marco (Polo), he prefers offbeat and adventurous travel.

MARK EVELEIGH has worked on Lonely Planet guidebooks on four continents, but when he's not on assignment he can often be found hiking in Spain. After trekking 761 miles (1225km) for his travel book *Vagabond: A Hiker's Homage to Rural Spain*, he continued for another 435 miles (700km), covering Lonely Planet's guide to the Camino de Santiago. Find him at @markeveleigh on Instagram.

NERISSA GOLDEN is editor of *Discover Montserrat* and a storyteller drawn to places shaped by culture, reinvention and rhythm. An island-hopper since birth, and with firmly Caribbean roots, her curiosity now carries her far beyond its shores. She writes about travel that invites discovery – from hidden island corners to unexpected global landscapes. Her ongoing goal? Chasing meaningful experiences, one festival, coastline and conversation at a time.

OLIVER SMITH is an award winning travel journalist based in London. For 10 years he traveled the world working for *Lonely Planet Magazine*. His first narrative travel book *On a Holy Island: A Modern Pilgrimage Across Britain* sets out to radically reframe our idea of 'pilgrimage' in Britain by retracing sacred travel made across time, and was published in March 2024 by Bloomsbury in the UK and Pegasus in the USA. Find him at @olismithtravel on Instagram.

PIA PETERSON HAGGARTY is the Photo Director at Lonely Planet. Previously, she was a features photo editor at *The Wall Street Journal*, photo editor at BuzzFeed News and a photo assistant at the *New York Times Magazine*. She's based in Brooklyn, New York.

PIERA CHEN is an anglophone writer and translator from Hong Kong, currently based in Taipei. She has co-authored some 20 travel guidebooks for Lonely Planet. Piera has a BA (liberal arts) from Pomona College, majoring in literature, and an MA in literary and cultural studies from the University of Hong Kong. She believes that if writing is the most disembodied of the arts, travel writing and poetry are the genres that make it less so. This is why she loves both. pierachen.com

PRACHI JOSHI is a Mumbai-based independent travel and food writer (and a photography enthusiast). Her favorite kind of trip involves a fun city break with plenty of art, culture and great food, followed by some relaxation in nature. When she's not writing, you'll find her in a cafe sipping espressos, people-watching and plotting her next trip. Follow her at @delishdirection on Instagram.

REBECCA WALLWORK is a writer based in Miami Beach, where tracking hotel openings is her favorite sport. She loves dogs, books, art deco, cabins in the woods and rambling around cities and coastal towns. Outside of travel journalism, she's a fiction writer and the author of a book on NKOTB's *Hangin' Tough*. Find her via rebeccawallwork.com @msrebeccaw on Instagram.

REGIS ST. LOUIS, the son of two Coloradans, has long been drawn to mountain wilderness. He has spent the past two decades writing about Alaska and other far-flung corners of the globe for Lonely Planet, and his research has taken him across six different continents. On his most recent trip north, he went sea kayaking amid glacial lagoons off Seward, hiked up snowy peaks near Denali and spotted countless moose on Southcentral's back roads. Follow him at @regisstlouis on Instagram.

ROBERT ISENBERG is a writer and filmmaker based in Rhode Island. He spent two happy years living and working as a journalist in Central America. An avid cyclist, Robert is always looking for new roads and trails to explore. He documents his travels on his vlog *You Are Here*.

SANDIE KESTELL spent six years living in Germany and working as a translator before joining Lonely Planet in 2016, where she's now Destination Editor for Central & Eastern Europe. Though most passionate about exploring German-speaking Europe and Europe's easternmost reaches, she loves traveling to new places. When she's not commissioning guidebooks, you can find her skiing in the Alps, hiking and baking.

SARAH GILBERT is a globetrotting freelance travel writer based in London. She's visited 80 countries and counting, searching for semi-habituated gorillas in Uganda, sampling llama jerky in Bolivia and scaling volcanoes in Nicaragua, all in the name of work. Destinations for Lonely Planet include two of her all-time favorite countries, Costa Rica and Morocco. And when she's not writing about wild nature, culture and conservation, she's planning her next trip. Find her at @sarahgtravels on Instagram.

SARAH REID is an award-winning Australian freelance travel writer and editor with a passion for adventure and regenerative travel. She has traveled to more than 130 countries in search of untold stories to share with the world's leading travel titles, but also loves yarning about her own backyard in northern New South Wales. Read her work at sarahreid.com.au and follow her adventures at @sarahreidtravels on Instagram.

SELENA TAKIGAWA HOY is Lonely Planet's Destination Editor for Northeast Asia and lives in Tokyo, a busy city that requires plenty of energy. For respite, she likes to rove the Japanese countryside staying in hot-spring inns.

SERINA PATEL grew up in San Diego and lived in Italy and Switzerland before returning to California and ultimately settling in Brooklyn, New York. For the past eight years, she's traveled extensively, always on the hunt for the best pastry in every city she visits. By day, she oversees Webby Award–winning email campaigns and programming; off the clock, she's baking sourdough and planning her next adventure.

ZARA SEKHAVATI is a half-Iranian award-winning writer. She's written for *The Telegraph*, the *Financial Times*, *The Sunday Times*, The Independent, *National Geographic Traveller* and *Wanderlust*. She writes about Iran on her website to show alternative stories about the country, away from the headlines. She is Lonely Planet's Destination Editor for the Middle East & North Africa. anotheriran.com

Photo Credits

Cover: Image Professionals GmbH/Alamy, mauritius images GmbH/Alamy, trabantos/Shutterstock, Ippei Naoi/Getty Images; **4:** Violette Franchi; **7:** Thitisan; **8:** KPG-Payless/Shutterstock; **11:** MxTravel/Shutterstock, Ippei Naoi/Getty Images; **12:** Richie Chan/Shutterstock, Anna Rasmussen; **13:** Sam DCruz; **14:** Joel Balsam; **17:** BrianPIrwin/Shutterstock, turtix/Shutterstock; **18:** Sarah Carlson Images/Shutterstock; **19:** Kit Leong/Shutterstock; **20:** trabantos/Shutterstock; **21:** Marek Slusarczyk/Alamy; **23:** Simun Galic/Shutterstock, Magdanatka/Shutterstock; **24:** Ivan Klindic/ Shutterstock; **25:** trabantos/Shutterstock; **26:** Audrius Venclova/Shutterstock; **28:** James Pham; **29:** James Pham; **30:** James Pham; **31:** James Pham; **32:** Jiri Viehmann/Shutterstock; **35:** LaniVC/ Shutterstock, Alex Cimbal/Shutterstock; **36:** Janelle Lugge/Shutterstock, Alex Cimbal/Shutterstock; **37:** James D. Morgan/Getty Images; **38:** lemaret pierrick/Shutterstock; **40:** Pierrick Lemaret/Getty Images; **41:** lemaret pierrick/Shutterstock, JHVEPhoto/Shutterstock; **42:** Artem Firsov/Alamy, Zoltan Bagosi/Alamy; **43:** Saowakhon Brown/GettyImages; **44:** Ainara Garcia/Alamy; **45:** Fotos593/Shutterstock; **47:** INTREEGUE Photography, robertharding/Alamy; **48:** Julien Capmeil, Rob Francis/Alamy; **49:** Jon Arnold Images Ltd/Alamy; **50:** Claudio Divizia/Shutterstock; **52:** Angelo Hornak/Alamy; **53:** Imago/Alamy, Animaflora PicsStock/Shutterstock; **54:** Simlinger/ Shutterstock; **55:** travelpix/Alamy; **56:** Dan MacKinnon/Shutterstock; **57:** mauritius images GmbH/ Alamy; **59:** Robert Wyatt/Alamy, catherine marois; **60:** Caroline Trefler, imageBROKER.com/Alamy; **61:** Devon Metcalf; **62:** Jon Bilous/Shutterstock; **63:** Kyle Myles; **64:** Jon Bilous/Shutterstock; **65:** Jon Bilous/Shutterstock, Sara Cottle; **66:** Kyle Myles, Jon Bilous/Shutterstock; **67:** David Miller Star/Shutterstock; **68:** Alison Etcheverry Images/Shutterstock; **71:** ByDroneVideos/Shutterstock, Marcos Radicella/GettyImages; **72:** Matyas Rehak/Shutterstock, Diego Grandi/Alamy; **73:** stacyarturogi/Shutterstock; **74:** saiko3p/Shutterstock; **76:** imageBROKER.com/Alamy; **77:** EQRoy/ Alamy, www.marcobrivio.photo/Shutterstock; **78:** Alexey Fedorenko/Shutterstock; **79:** Anton_ Ivanov/Shutterstock; **80:** LP2 Studio/Shutterstock; **83:** Tuul & Bruno Morandi/GettyImages; **84:** Takatoshi Kurikawa/Alamy, Heng Yu; **85:** Brian Finke; **86:** Tomacrosse/Shutterstock; **88:** Heavenlyflower/Shutterstock; **89:** travellinglight/Alamy, ROA via Keteleer Gallery; **90:** Tonia Kraakman; **91:** byvalet/Shutterstock; **92:** David Kleyn; **93:** Mauritius Images GmbH; **95:** Maxi Perez, Nadezhda Bolotina/Shutterstock; **96:** Jaroslav Hruska/Shutterstock, Botond Horvath/ Shutterstock; **97:** WINDCOLORS/Shutterstock; **98:** Damsea/Shutterstock 100: Tim Cook 101: Dmitry Burlakov/Shutterstock, PaNaPrO/Shutterstock 102: robertharding/Shutterstock 103: Rainer Lesniewski/Shutterstock 104: Hemis/Alamy; **105:** Hyserb/Shutterstock; **107:** Hamza Makhchoune/ Shutterstock, Hyserb/Shutterstock; **108:** Richard Sharrocks/Getty Images, robertharding/ Shutterstock; **109:** Kadagan/Shutterstock; **110:** MehmetO/Shutterstock; **112:** Mithun Malakar/ Shutterstock; **113:** AjayTvm/Shutterstock, Sumit Bhowmick/Shutterstock; **114:** WIND WATCHERS/ Shutterstock, Unforgettable.Moments/Shutterstock; **115:** Hnjosh/Shutterstock; **116:** Pia Peterson Haggarty; **117:** Pia Peterson Haggarty; **119:** Pia Peterson Haggarty; **120:** Pia Peterson Haggarty; **121:** Pia Peterson Haggarty; **122:** Alexi Hobbs; **124:** Alexi Hobbs; **125:** Alexi Hobbs, Shawn.ccf/Alamy; **126:** Stephanie Foden; **127:** Mario Beauregard Beaustock/Alamy; **128:** Nancy Borowick; **131:** Mark Read; **132:** Nancy Borowick; **133:** Nancy Borowick; **134:** Becca Hunt; **135:** Phillip Bindeman/500px; **136:** Dan the Man Man/Shutterstock; **137:** Becca Hunt; **138:** Jim_Brown_Photography/ Shutterstock; **139:** Yaya Ernst; **140:** Hamdan Yoshida/Shutterstock 141: philipus/Alamy; **143:** SOman92/Shutterstock, Justin Foulkes for Lonely Planet; **144:** Glen Berlin/Shutterstock, Simone Augstburger/Shutterstock; **145:** Westend61 on Offset; **146:** Cavan Images - Offset/Shutterstock; **148:** Eugen Haag/Shutterstock; **149:** Mongkolchon Akesin/Shutterstock, kyslynskaha/ Shutterstockl; **150:** John Warburton-Lee Photography/Alamy; **151:** Marius Dobilas/Shutterstock; **152:** Jessica Lockhart; **155:** Jessica Lockhart; **156:** Jessica Lockhart; **157:** Jessica Lockhart; **159:** MiraSid; **160:** one-image photography/Alamy; **162:** Becky Duffy/Shutterstock; **163:** Jeremy L Fratkin; **164:** Ashley Cooper pics/Alamy, Jeremy L Fratkin; **165:** Jeremy L Fratkin; **166:** Yiorgis Yerolymbos via Department of Culture and Tourism – Abu Dhabi; **169:** Mohamed Somji; **170:** Courtesy of Natural History Museum Abu Dhabi, Courtesy of Natural History Museum Abu Dhabi;

171: Mohamed Somji; **172:** GummyBone/GettyImages; **173:** Jacob Boomsma//Shutterstock; **174:** wildnerdpix/Alamy; **175:** Steve Apps/Alamy, Alisha Bube/GettyImages; **176:** Sean Pavone/ Shutterstock; **177:** Tribune Content Agency LLC/Alamy; **178:** Anita Nicholson/Alamy; **181:** Will Perrett/GettyImages, jimmonkphotography/Shutterstock; **182:** Dave Head/Shutterstock, Binson Calfort/Shutterstock; **183:** Umomos/Shutterstock; **184:** Serina Patel; **186:** Serina Patel; **187:** Serina Patel, Mikel Dabbah/Shutterstock; **188:** Serina Patel, Serina Patel; **189:** Serina Patel; **190:** Courtesy of 1 Hotel, Courtesy of Goodtime Hotel; **191:** Courtesy of 1 Hotel; **192:** Austin John via; **193:** Courtesy of Goodtime Hotel, Courtesy of Goodtime Hotel; **194:** Courtesy of 1 Hotel, Claudia Uribe Touri (Courtesy of the Standard); **195:** Courtesy of 1 Hotel; **196:** Violette Franchi; **198:** Violette Franchi; **199:** Violette Franchi, Philip Lee Harvey; **200:** Violette Franchi; **201:** katatonia82; **202:** Anup Shah/GettyImages; **205:** Danita Delimont/Alamy, John Giustina/GettyImages; **206:** Imago/ Alamy, Josemar Franco/Shutterstock; **207:** guenterguni/GettyImages; **208:** Bhaswaran Bhattacharya/Alamy; **210:** Juliet FergusonAlamy; **211:** Image Source LimitedAlamy, Dave PattisonAlamy; **212:** ZUMA Press Inc, Image Source Limited; **213:** Dinodia PhotosAlamy; **214:** Ed Goodacre/Shutterstock; **215:** flashgun/Shutterstock; **217:** Martin Valigursky/Shutterstock, Ramunas Bruzas/Alamy; **218:** corners74/Shutterstock, peacefoo/Shutterstock; **219:** Greg Balfour Evans/ Alamy; **220:** Sybille Reuter/Shutterstock; **223:** Seahorse Dive Center, PADI; **224:** Aerial-motion/ Shutterstock; **225:** Brandee Anthony, Zeke Motta; **226:** Paulina Szklarska/Shutterstock; **229:** efenzi/GettyImages, Vaclav Sebek/Shutterstock; **230:** Photo_Traveller/Shutterstock, STOCKEROcr/ Shutterstock; **231:** Cavan-Images/Shutterstock; **232:** Chris Moody; **234:** Lisette Rooney (Courtesy of Rose Island Lighthouse and Fort Hamilton Trust); **235:** Corey Favino, Chris Moody; **236:** Lisette Rooney (Courtesy of Rose Island Lighthouse and Fort Hamilton Trust); **237:** Corey Favino; **238:** Collab Media/Shutterstock; **239:** Parilov/Shutterstock; **241:** Xinhua News Agency/Getty Images, evgenykz/Shutterstock via Akimat of Astana City; **242:** Qazaq Gourmet, ppl/Shutterstock; **243:** Sembi Production; **244:** Mlenny/Getty Images; **245:** Fred Pompermayer; **246:** JohanLetang/ Shutterstock; **247:** Jessica Lockhart, Damsea/Shutterstock; **248:** Evgeny Vasenev; **249:** Jessica Lockhart; **250:** Kehinde Temitope Odutayo/Shutterstock; **253:** Cesar J. Pollo/Shutterstock, Rachel Torres/Alamy; **254:** Xinovap/Shutterstock, Wirestock, Inc./Alamy; **255:** Xinovap/Shutterstock; **256:** Benny Marty/Shutterstock; **258:** Regis St Louis; **259:** Regis St Louis, Regis St Louis; **260:** Regis St Louis, Talkeetna Air Taxi; **261:** Regis St Louis; **262:** Image Professionals GmbH/Alamy; **263:** F. Rubino/Shutterstock; **265:** Gareth McCormack/Alamy, Clare Hargreaves/Alamy; **266:** noel bennett/ Alamy, Dennis Frates/Alamy; **267:** Greens and Blues/Shutterstock; **268:** Lisa Wynne; **269:** Lisa Wynne; **270:** GAGAnuma/Shutterstock; **271:** Pangni/Shutterstock, Lisa Wynne; **272:** Andrew Bain/ Alamy; **273:** Lisa Wynne; **274:** Marina Calderon; **277:** Marina Calderon, Gianfranco Vivi/ Shutterstock; **278:** Marina Calderon, AsiaTravel/Shutterstock; **279:** Marina Calderon; **280:** Patsperspektive/Shutterstock; **282:** Jessica Lockhart; **283:** Jessica Lockhart, SouthWestImagesAus/ Shutterstock; **284:** Marianna Massey/GettyImages, Jessica Lockhart; **285:** James D. Morgan/ GettyImages; **286:** Amy Perez; **287:** Shelly Perry; **289:** Michal Hamet/Shutterstock, Bjarn Bronsveld; **290:** Andres Medina, Kike Arnaiz; **291:** Fagner Andrade/Shutterstock; **292:** annaj77/ Shutterstock; **293:** Imam Moolono/Shutterstock; **294:** Piera Chen, Bildagentur-online/Getty Images; **295:** Piera Chen; **296:** Piera Chen; **297:** LEOCHEN66/Shutterstock; **298:** Carolina2009/ Shutterstock; **300:** Solomakha/Shutterstock; **301:** Dayyan Armstrong; **302:** Dayyan Armstrong, Frank Lambert/Shutterstock; **303:** Dayyan Armstrong; **304:** Constantine Johnny/Alamy; **306:** Abang Faizul/Shutterstock; **307:** aparajitha joseph/Shutterstock, dave stamboulis/Alamy; **308:** Dave Stamboulis/GettyImages, Junior Chin/Shutterstock; **309:** Nature Picture Library/Alamy

Index

N

O

P

Q

R

S

T

Best in Travel 2027
Project Editors Becca Hunt, Polly Thomas
Designer Emily Dubin
Publishing Director Piers Pickard
Publisher Becca Hunt
Creative Direction Emily Dubin
Print Production Nigel Longuet

September 2026
Published by Lonely Planet Global Limited
CRN: 554153
ISBN: 978 18065 3435 7

10 9 8 7 6 5 4 3 2 1
Printed in Malaysia

STAY IN TOUCH
lonelyplanet.com/contact

Lonely Planet Global Limited
Digital Depot, Roe Lane (off Thomas St),
Digital Hub, Dublin 8,
D08 TCV4
Ireland
(EU authorised representative)

FSC
www.fsc.org
MIX
Paper | Supporting responsible forestry
FSC™ C021741

Paper in this book is certified against the Forest Stewardship Council™ standards. FSC™ promotes environmentally responsible, socially beneficial and economically viable management of the world's forests.